WSS

THE MAKING OF THE

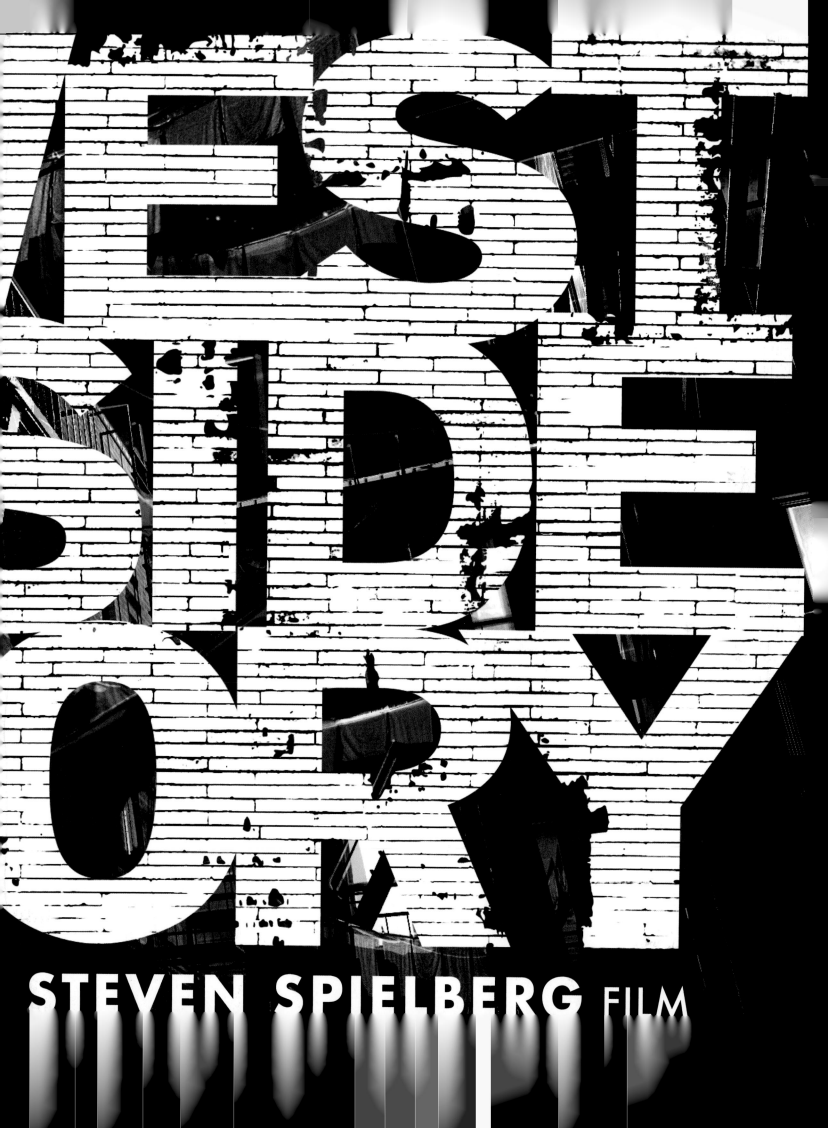

CONTENTS

Title page
Concept art by Alexios Chrysikos

This page
Ariana DeBose (Anita) and David Alvarez (Bernardo) in "America"

Following spread, top
Jets John Michael Fiumara (Big Deal), Jess LeProtto (A-Rab), My[l] (Snow Boy), Ben Cook (Mouthpiece), Kevin Csolak (Diesel), Patric[k] (Baby John), and Kyle Allen (Balkan) on the set of "Gee, Officer K[rupke"]

Following spread, bottom
Sharks Adriel Flete (Julito), Sebastian Serra (Braulio), Andrei C[.] (Jochi), David Alvarez (Bernardo), Ricardo A. Zayaz (Chago), and Anthony Rubio (Quique) sing "La Borinqueña"

INTRODUCTION

IN 2019, Steven Spielberg announced that he would tackle a full-length musical for the first time and revisit the all-time classic *West Side Story*. For someone like me who has been documenting Steven's cinema for more than twenty-seven years, this was an occasion I didn't want to miss.

Being "invited to the dance," and witnessing the making of the film firsthand, from early rehearsals to production to the final orchestra recordings, was, to say the least, an unforgettable experience for everyone involved. The excitement on set was palpable; there was a real sense of an event happening. Not only did it feel like a film of cinematic importance, one that challenged a director who never ceases to push the boundaries of visual language, but it also presented screenwriter Tony Kushner the chance to adapt the story for our times. Although it is still set in the fifties, this is an all-new vision of *West Side Story*. Alongside Spielberg, Kushner is to be celebrated and applauded for making the script his own and for giving it a sense of urgency that could not be more fitting for our current climate.

Watching the actors/singers/dancers—the so-called triple threats—embrace the platform that Steven created for them with his creative team was exhilarating. The performances, as well as the friendships created offscreen, made every day of filming a celebration of the legacy of one of the greatest musicals ever created, and confirmed how much it is still able to speak to new generations.

Being in the privileged position of documenting the film behind the scenes and conducting close to one hundred interviews, I quickly realized that there was an opportunity to share the oral history of this spectacular film in book form, through personal stories that only those behind and in front of the camera could tell. Illustrated with the artful unit photography of Niko Tavernese, as well as storyboards, costume concept illustrations, and behind-the scenes images, this book takes readers on a journey, not unlike the one experienced by everyone who worked on the film. As many of us know, however, a film is not shot in the order in which it is written. For clarity, the interview quotes are organized to highlight the history of the project first, and then each subsequent section is presented in the order in which the musical numbers appear in the context of the new story. One could, in fact, easily imagine listening to the cast recording while reading the book for maximum effect.

For Steven Spielberg, making *West Side Story* was the adventure of a lifetime— and the realization of a dream; a celebration of diversity through art. It is an honor to now pass the narrative of this volume over to the incredible cast and crew of this film to tell, in their own voices, how they came together to create Steven Spielberg's new film version of *West Side Story*.

LAURENT BOUZEREAU
May 2021

WEST SIDE STORY
A STEVEN SPIELBERG FILM

Executive Producers
RITA MORENO, DANIEL LUPI,
ADAM SOMNER, TONY KUSHNER
Produced by STEVEN SPIELBERG, p.g.a.
KRISTIE MACOSKO KRIEGER, p.g.a. KEVIN McCOLLUM
Original Choreography by JEROME ROBBINS
Chroeographed by JUSTIN PECK
Based on the Stage Play, Book by ARTHUR LAURENTS,
Music by LEONARD BERNSTEIN, Lyrics by STEPHEN SONDHEIM,
Play Conceived, Directed, and Choreographed by JEROME ROBBINS
Lyrics by STEPHEN SONDHEIM, Music by LEONARD BERNSTEIN,
Screenplay by TONY KUSHNER, Directed by STEVEN SPIELBERG

WHO'S WHO IN THE CAST

Tony	ANSEL ELGORT
María	RACHEL ZEGLER
Anita	ARIANA DeBOSE
Bernardo	DAVID ALVAREZ
Valentina	RITA MORENO
Officer Krupke	BRIAN D'ARCY JAMES
Lieutenant Schrank	COREY STOLL
Riff	MIKE FAIST
Chino	JOSH ANDRÉS RIVERA
Anybodys	EZRA MENAS

SHARKS

Aníbal	DAVID AVILÉS MORALES
Braulio	SEBASTIAN SERRA
Chago	RICARDO A. ZAYAS
Chucho	CARLOS E. GONZALEZ
Flaco	RICKY UBEDA
Jochi	ANDREI CHAGAS
Julito	ADRIEL FLETE
Junior	JACOB GUZMAN
Manolo	KELVIN DELGADO
Pipo	CARLOS SÁNCHEZ FALÚ
Quique	JULIUS ANTHONY RUBIO
Sebas	YUREL ECHEZARRETA
Tino	DAVID GUZMAN

Top
Sebastion Serra (Braulio) and
Melody Martí (Pili)

Middle
Halli Toland (Sweden) and Daniel
Patrick Russel (Little Molly

Bottom
Talia Ryder (Tessa)
and Patrick Higgins (Baby John

JETS

Action	SEAN HARRISON JONES
A-Rab	JESS LePROTTO
Baby John	PATRICK HIGGINS
Balkan	KYLE ALLEN
Big Deal	JOHN MICHAEL FIUMARA
Diesel	KEVIN CSOLAK
Ice	KYLE COFFMAN
Little Moly	DANIEL PATRICK RUSSELL
Mouthpiece	BEN COOK
Numbers	HARRISON COLL
Skink	GARETT HAWE
Snowboy	MYLES ERLICK
Tiger	JULIAN ELIA

SHARK GIRLS

Charita	TANAIRI SADE VAZQUEZ
Clary	YESENIA AYALA
Conchi	GABRIELA M. SOTO
Cuca	JULIETTE FELICIANO ORTIZ
Ili	JEANETTE DELGADO
Isa	MARIA ALEXIS RODRIGUEZ
Jacinta	EDRIZ E. ROSA PÉREZ
Luz	ILDA MASON
Montse	JENNIFER FLORENTINO
Pili	MELODY MARTÍ
Rosalía	ANA ISABELLE
Tati	GABY DIAZ
Tere	ISABELLA WARD

JET GIRLS

Dot	ELOISE KROPP
Graziella	PALOMA GARCIA-LEE
Gussie	LEIGH-ANN ESTY
Karen	LAUREN LEACH
Mack	BRITTANY POLLACK
Mamie	KELLIE DROBNICK
Maxie	SKYE MATTOX
Natalie	ADRIANA PIERCE
Rhonda	JONALYN SAXER
Sorella	BRIANNA ABRUZZO
Sweden	HALLI TOLAND
Tat	SARA ESTY
Tessa	TALIA RYDER
Velma	MADDIE ZIEGLER

David Guzman (Tino) and
Yesenia Ayala (Clary)

Ricky Ubeda (Flaco)
and his dog, Fofo!

Ezra Menas (Anybodys)

LEGACY

TONY KUSHNER (screenwriter/executive producer): Steven is an artist, first and foremost. Everything he makes comes from a deep personal place; there's great heart in his work, along with the technical brilliance; there's an enormous empathic imagination, curiosity about other people's lives, and an abiding passion for democracy and justice. And he knows what artists know: that he needs to set himself new challenges with every film; he's always eager to try something new, something difficult, something he's never done before, something that scares him.

STEVEN SPIELBERG (director/producer): I've never directed a film musical, though there are musical numbers in some of my movies—for example, in *Indiana Jones and the Temple of Doom*, or a comedy like *1941*. In fact, the most satisfying thing about the entire production of *1941* was shooting the jitterbug dance contest that Paul De Rolf choreographed for me. I had never shot a musical number before, though I'd been a big fan of the Busby Berkeley musicals. I wasn't trying to rival those, but I wanted to experience what it was like to direct a song-and-dance number. It took three days to shoot it—and to me those were the best three days out of the entire 178 shooting days it took to make *1941*.

Opening *Indiana Jones and the Temple of Doom* with a musical number was George Lucas's idea. He said, "Hey, Steven, you always say you want to shoot musicals. You're a frustrated musical director!" So, we put together this crazy number based on Cole Porter's "Anything Goes," and Danny Daniels choreographed it.

My mother played the piano, and music was a great love of both my parents. My sisters and I grew up listening to my mom's repertoire: Schuman, Beethoven, Brahms,

musical theater works by American composers, and that's *Porgy and Bess* (1935). And even though *West Side Story* isn't through-composed, even though it has a book and lyrics rather than a libretto, I'd argue that is every bit as much of a grand opera as Gershwin's masterpiece.

So I started trying to get meetings with the rights holders and keepers of the *West Side Story* flame. Theater producer Kevin McCollum, who'd produced the most recent Broadway revival, broke the ice for me and my team and gave us some great advice on logistically how we could get another film version of *West Side Story* made alongside all the rightsholders—especially since the first film is such a landmark in the history of movie musicals. We met with David Saint, representing Arthur Laurents [1917–2011; writer of the original Broadway production's book]; Nina, Jamie, and Alexander Bernstein, Leonard Bernstein's [1918–1990; composer of the music for the original Broadway production and director of the New York Philharmonic] children; and the trustees from the Jerome Robbins estate [1918–1998; director and choreographer of the original Broadway production], and I told them about my passion for the musical and some of my early ideas, and all the meetings went well, but I really didn't know how it would go. I waited while the estates' representatives and Stephen Sondheim [lyricist for the original Broadway production] discussed what they wanted to do, and I tried to prepare

Chopin, and Shostakovich. I think it was her love of music, combined with my insatiable appetite to understand everything about movies and movie making, that led me to start collecting motion picture soundtrack albums when I was young, around ten or eleven years old. I'm not sure who got the soundtrack album for *West Side Story*, or if my parents had already bought the Broadway cast album before the film was released, but I know I loved it the first time I listened to it. As a kid I could sing every one of its songs by heart—and I did sing them, at dinner, till I wore out the patience of everybody in my family. The score feels like it's always been part of my DNA. I didn't know how, exactly, but it's always seemed inevitable to me that eventually I'd find some way to work on *West Side Story*.

I've been looking for a musical to adapt and direct for many years, and I've considered a number of possibilities, but I kept coming back to *West Side Story*. I think it has only one peer among

Above
Producer Kristie Macosko Krieger

Opposite
Steven Spielberg introduces Mike Faist (Riff) to Russ Tamblyn (Riff in the 1961 film version of *West Side Story*).

myself to be turned down. So it was an amazing day when I heard that everyone involved had given me the go-ahead, meaning that I could tell Tony Kushner to move forward with writing the script. Once David Saint felt confident that Tony and I wanted a screenplay that was built on and that would honor the spirit of Arthur Laurents's brilliant book, he gave us tremendous latitude and permission to explore, to return to some of Arthur's original impulses, and to reimagine certain aspects of the story. When he delivered the script, I knew that Tony's version was the *West Side Story* I'd waited to direct.

KRISTIE MACOSKO KRIEGER (producer): Many people knew that Steven wanted to direct a musical, and was interested in reimagining *West Side Story*, but we didn't start seriously exploring the possibility

of securing the rights for it until 2014. We approached the project with great humility and the respect that such an iconic piece deserves. We owe a lot to Kevin McCollum and Emma Watts at what was 20th Century Fox, now part of Disney, who guided us through this journey. Personally, I knew this would be an enormous challenge, because neither Steven nor I had tackled a musical before. But *West Side Story* is the kind of project you dream about, and we were thrilled to embark on what we knew would be a very special and important film. From beginning to end, the entire process took about six years, with almost four years focused on preproduction, four months of filming, and roughly six months of post-production work.

STEPHEN SONDHEIM (lyricist): I had written the score for an unproduced show called

Saturday Night, and a producer named Martin Gabel asked me to audition for a musical called *Serenade*, based on the James Cain novel. It was going to have music by Leonard Bernstein, direction by Jerome Robbins, and a book by Arthur Laurents. The project soon was canceled; then maybe a year and a half later I was at an opening-night party and there was Arthur Laurents. He told me he was writing a musical based on *Romeo and Juliet* with music by Leonard Bernstein and directed by Jerry Robbins . . . that same group. I asked who was doing the lyrics. He explained that originally Betty Comden and Adolph Green were going to do it, but they had an agreement they couldn't get out of. He proceeded to say that he wasn't all that impressed with my

music but thought my lyrics were terrific. He invited me to come and play for Bernstein, and I got the job. By then, Arthur had done a three-page outline, and so it all began. I was twenty-five.

At that time, I wanted to write music, and I was reluctant to be involved with writing lyrics only. My mentor was Oscar Hammerstein; he had been a surrogate father to me, and he taught me most of what I know about musical theater. It was he who advised me to take the job. He told me I would learn a lot working with this group. And he was right.

ANSEL ELGORT (Tony): My dad is a photographer, a lover of art and music and of Leonard Bernstein. My mother actually worked

Above
From left: Steven Spielberg, Deborah Borda (CEO of the New York Philharmonic), Nina Bernstein Simmons, Alexander Bernstein, and conductor Gustavo Dudamel

with Bernstein when she choreographed his opera *A Quiet Place*. I grew up on the Upper West Side of New York City, and there were pictures in our home of who I thought was my grandfather, my dad's father. I never knew him, but it turned out they were, in fact, photos of Leonard Bernstein. My whole life I thought Leonard Bernstein was my grandfather! And now, he might as well be.

JAMIE BERNSTEIN (daughter of Leonard Bernstein): When I was four years old, it was very common for me to walk past my father's studio off the front hall of our apartment on Fifty-Seventh Street.

I would peek through the door—and through a blue haze of cigarette smoke, I could just about make out my father, hard at work with Jerry Robbins, Arthur Laurents, and Steve Sondheim, on what became *West Side Story*.

DAVID SAINT (literary executor, Arthur Laurents's estate): The whole saga of *West Side Story* is like *Rashomon*, because so many people have different versions of what they think the origins of it were. And you can listen to them all and not believe any of them. Or believe whatever you choose to believe. But Arthur Laurents, who wrote the book [the script/narrative structure of a musical] for the show, was always a fighter for social justice. He said in his lifetime "the three lowest ones on the ladder were being African American, gay, and Jewish, and I'm two out of three." He was always

fighting for the marginalized in society and for social justice. And so he wanted to write a show with that theme and zeroed in on the Jewish and Catholic rivalries on the Lower East Side. But as he said to Jerome Robbins, with whom he was talking this through and forming it, he realized there already was *Abie's Irish Rose*, which had been a big hit on Broadway in the twenties and revived in 1937 and 1954. That story was already told. They put it aside. Arthur then talked about being by the pool in Los Angeles and reading about gang wars with the Latino community and relating the same situation to New York. There were all these reports of violence on both coasts. Arthur said to Jerry, "Let's make our musical about the Puerto Ricans and the whites on the Upper West Side, not on the Lower East Side." And hence, what started as *East Side Story* became *West Side Story*.

JAMIE BERNSTEIN: My father used his music to express the story by writing Latin-Caribbean music for the Sharks and bebop jazz for the Jets. It's just amazing to think back to the time when he was working on *West Side Story*, because even though that was a gigantic, daunting enterprise, it was only one of several things that he was doing at the same time. He was writing a whole other show, *Candide*, with a completely different, European flavor. He was also pursuing his conducting career, and just about the time *West Side Story* opened was the same moment that he took over as the music director of the New York Philharmonic. And so he was going back and forth between being a conductor and a composer, both of which were peaking simultaneously.

ALEXANDER BERNSTEIN (son of Leonard Bernstein): My father loved Latin music. He had spent time in Florida Keys; he'd been to Mexico a few times. He listened to the radio down there and would hear Cuban and Puerto Rican music stations. He loved the rhythm, and it's all there, in *West Side Story*. And the same with the jazz aspect of the score. He loved jazz and listened to it all the time and would go to clubs. You can feel both influences in his composition of *West Side Story*.

NINA BERNSTEIN SIMMONS (daughter of Leonard Bernstein): My father was writing *Candide* and *West Side Story* simultaneously. He would shelve one to work on the other and then vice versa, and actually there was a bit of cross-pollination between the two shows. One of the songs, "Krupke," in an earlier incarnation was meant for *Candide*. It didn't quite work in *Candide*, so it moved over to *West Side Story*. Same with "One Hand, One Heart."

JOHN WILLIAMS (music consultant): I first met Lenny [Leonard Bernstein] in Boston in the 1980s when we shared a number of concerts commemorating such events as the Harvard Commencement and the hundredth anniversary

Above
Stephen Sondheim visits with Steven Spielberg.

Opposite
(top) Jamie Bernstein (bottom) Ellen Sorrin, director of the Jerome Robbins Foundation and a trustee of the Robbins Rights Trust

of the Boston Symphony. I also saw him at Tanglewood very often through the years, and he was always greatly supportive and encouraging of me.

I think without question our mid-twentieth-century American musical life would have been very dull without Lenny. His greatest gift certainly was as a teacher and communicator. As a composer, his work for the theater, particularly pieces like *On the Town*, *Chichester Psalms*, *West Side Story*, and *Candide*, likely will be his most enduring. As a young conductor, his work could seem tense and taut, often overshadowed by his innate charisma and theatricality. However, with age he matured, placing him among some of the great orchestral conductors of the period, including Claudio Abbado, Zubin Mehta, and Daniel Barenboim.

DAVID SAINT: Arthur always liked to summarize all of his work in one sentence. For him, *West Side Story* was simply the struggle to love in a world of bigotry and violence. Without the love story, the bigotry and violence aspects of the plot wouldn't work, and vice versa.

JAMIE BERNSTEIN: All four creators of *West Side Story* were gay or bisexual—and that feeling of "being different" was an element that they didn't completely express in their personal life but was definitely part of the subtext of *West Side Story*.

ELLEN SORRIN (trustee, Jerome Robbins Foundation/Robbins Rights Trust): Jerome Robbins both directed and choreographed *West Side Story*. His credit actually was "Conceived, Directed, and Choreographed by Jerome Robbins," and it was put in a box on the poster. It really stood out, and he wanted the recognition. He felt a great deal of ownership. But to anyone who doesn't know anything about him, I would say that he was one of the great artists of the twentieth century. I would also say that he created work that is part of our culture, and that anyone interested in America should see his work. Jerry's great gift was the fact that he told

stories through choreography. I don't think anyone had really done that before him. And it came very naturally. If you look at the dance numbers in *West Side Story*, they really tell the story. They move the story along.

JULIO MONGE (consultant on Puerto Rican culture and history): At the time I knew Jerome Robbins, he was turning seventy years old, and I had moved to New York from Puerto Rico. Mr. Robbins was coming back to Broadway after twenty years of absence for a show called *Jerome Robbins' Broadway*; it encompassed many of his pieces, including *West Side Story*. Peter Gennaro, who is rarely mentioned and is a great American dancer-choreographer and contributed immensely to the original Broadway show by choreographing almost all of the Latino dances, came to work with us.

DAVID SAINT: Through the prism of today, it's very tough to find another show as

brilliantly conceived on every level. Sometimes you get a great score and you don't get a great book.

Sometimes you get a good book and not a great score, not good lyrics, not good direction, not good choreography. To have it all is nearly miraculous.

STEPHEN SONDHEIM: It ran for a respectable year and a half on Broadway. It eventually made its money back and a small bit of profit, but it was by no means a big hit. It was, however, talked about a lot. *West Side Story* didn't change the theater; it was a unique piece and there was no reason for other shows to be influenced by it, since its only innovation was to show how dance coud be as much a part of storytelling as dialogue, music, and lyrics. It was a great example of content dictating form. The form of it evolved as we wrote it.

LARRY KAPLAN (unit publicist): I saw the original production of *West Side Story* on Broadway, in October 1957. I was sixteen and a half. My standing-room ticket cost about $1.75. It had the feeling of a big event; the audience reaction was rapturous. I remember the production vividly. "Dance at the Gym," "America," the "Quintet" live in my head. I can see clearly, even now, Larry Kert and Carol Lawrence, who played Tony and María, on that fire escape, and hear their melding voices spinning a melody of celestial beauty.

Some other details are blurred now by having

Above
David Saint, literary executor, Arthur Laurents's estate

Opposite
Steven Spielberg and Julian Elia (Tiger, right) meet David Bean, who played Tiger in the 1961 film and has a cameo in this new version of *West Side Story*.

seen so many different versions of the material, but the original performances by Larry Kert, Carol Lawrence, Chita Rivera, and Michael Callan are indelible. I became a serial offender. Standing room was cheap. I saw the show seven times before it closed.

STEPHEN SONDHEIM: We had discussed the possibilities of a film version among ourselves. And then, suddenly, it was happening. I was not around for the shooting, but I made some lyric changes. I remember hearing the producer say, "We've been shooting with Jerry [Robbins] for two weeks, and we're four weeks behind."

RITA MORENO (Anita, original film version; executive producer/Valentina, new film): I met Jerome Robbins on *The*

King and I, and it was really an extraordinary experience. He was brilliant. And then later, he asked me if I wanted to go to New York and audition for a play he was making called *West Side Story*. He explained it was a new version of *Romeo and Juliet*, and that I'd be wonderful for it. Yet, when it came down to it, I didn't have the guts to go for a Broadway show. But it was Robbins who told Robert Wise about me a few years later for the movie version. I auditioned for the singing, the acting, and then Jerry said, "You've got to audition for the dancing now. And if you don't cut the dancing, you don't get this part." I was very nervous, and I auditioned with Howard Jeffrey, who was Robbins's co-choreographer [credited as "Dance Assistant" in the film]. He could tell I hadn't danced in a while, but eventually, Jerry Robbins said, "She has a great sense of humor and style, and she is a fast learner." That's how I got the part.

RUSS TAMBLYN (original Riff, film version): Our original movie was certainly a classic. There's no question about that. But there were some flaws in it.

At the time, I was under contract at MGM Studios when this came up; they agreed to let me test for the film. I wanted to do the part of Tony. I tested with several girls. . . . I had the same agent as Bob Wise [the film's director], and so I kept checking in, saying, "Any word yet?" Finally, the agent called to say they gave the part to Richard Beymer. But they offered me Riff. I thought, *Oh my God, I don't think I can do that strong of dancing.* So actually, I learned how to dance on the job. Jerry Robbins explained how I would not do any acrobatics in the film because Riff is not a gymnast. He's just a dancer. It's straight dancing. It wasn't until Jerry was fired that Tony Mordente (who played Action in the film) said, "let's put some tumbling in."

The young actors in this new film are going to do a lot of roles in the future, but they're never going to get over being a Jet. It'll stick with them forever. I'm still in touch with the cast members, we have reunions and parties and we still get together.

JAMIE BERNSTEIN: My father did not love the movie. At the time it was made, he was very busy with his conducting career and turned the musical direction to an arranger by the name of Johnny Green and to his orchestrators, Sid Ramin and Irv Kostal. Ramin and Kostal were the ones who were on the set working on my father's behalf.

JOHN WILLIAMS: I remember in 1960 playing the piano during the orchestral recordings for the film version of *West Side Story*. The music was adapted for a large concert orchestra conducted by Johnny Green, which was quite a departure from the smaller orchestration done by Sid Ramin and Irwin Kostal for the original stage production. It was at these sessions that I met Ramin and Kostal; we became lifelong friends.

ELLEN SORRIN: There were a few things that Jerry never wanted to discuss, and being fired from the film was one of them. But I found out over the years that a lot of the work he did was already done by the time he was no longer involved. His imprint on the film is still very, very strong. And even though it won him an Oscar, which he shared with Robert Wise for Best Director, it had to have been a very painful time in his life.

RITA MORENO: Jerry Robbins was fired by the time we got to the "Mambo" at the gym, and we were all terribly upset. He was very hard on us, but we really felt his absence. There was a palpable difference after he left. Jerry was a dynamic force and presence. There was something about him that radiated tension— some of it negative, and some of it positive.

He was very demanding, and he did tons and tons of takes, which is why he was eventually fired. He wouldn't say, "Print it!" Even though the dancers were scared to death of him, they worshipped him.

VIRGINIA SÁNCHEZ KORROL (historical consultant): I saw the movie in 1961, and at that point in my life I was recently married. I had graduated from Brooklyn College and was an English teacher in a Chicago public high school. The day I went to see *West Side Story*, I had just completed a unit on *Romeo and Juliet*. Two things happened: One was that I immediately recognized the *Romeo and Juliet* story; the other was that I recognized myself in it. I had married a person who was not Puerto Rican. Families were up in arms; we left the city soon after we were married. But I'll never forget a letter I received from my sister at the time the film came out where she wrote, "Brooklyn College is great. All the guys want to date me. . . . They think I'm María from *West Side Story*!" That film marked the first time I saw New York Puerto Rican characters portrayed on-screen. It was a very significant event.

DAVID SAINT: The film came out in 1961, and most of the actors, except for Rita Moreno, were not Puerto Rican. Arthur didn't like that. Ironically, the immense success of the film worldwide made him a very rich and famous man.

RITA MORENO: For some reason, I was convinced the movie was going to be a major flop. The movie won ten Oscars. Winning Best Supporting Actress didn't really change my life; some things remain the same when you're Hispanic. I couldn't get another movie that wasn't about a gang. It was heartbreaking.

ELLEN SORRIN: We taped all of Jerry's rehearsals. In one of the rehearsals, he's talking to the Sharks and he points to the Jets and says, "They live badly. You live worse. I want to see that in your work." When he was rehearsing "America" with the girls, he said to them, "You all have your own stories, you all have your own clothes that you wear. You all have your own experiences. I want to see that in the work." He was always about the characters and went for the narrative. He wanted everyone to have their own motivation.

DAVID SAINT: I knew Arthur until he died, and he said to me, "I want you to promise me

that if they make another movie of *West Side Story*, you will fight to make sure it isn't done by a theater person. Theater is different than film. I want a cinematic genius to do it. And I want a writer who will respect what I wrote but also the *essence* of what I wrote." So, when this all started to happen and it came as a possibility that Steven Spielberg was interested, I went, *Well, check that off; he is that cinematic genius that Arthur wanted.* When I eventually met with Steven, we talked for a long time, and I was knocked out by his humility, how down-to-earth he is. Then Steven said he wanted to work with Tony Kushner. I thought, *Well, check that box as well,* not only because he is a genius writer, but he also was someone that Arthur truly admired.

STEVEN SPIELBERG: Those four guys [Leonard Bernstein, Arthur Laurents, Jerome Robbins, Stephen Sondheim] created a masterwork for the theater. It redefined

Broadway musicals, it was the first of its kind, utterly original, and no one can capture that kind of lightning-in-a-bottle twice. We understood that, but while we worked to honor this masterwork, to live up to its demands, we also hoped to try to find our way in to the energy and chutzpah it took to make something that new, that fresh. *West Side Story* is both incredibly assured, and also incredibly young. And also it's deeply true—about love and life and death. I wanted everyone on the creative team to feel part of bringing the profound and beautiful truths of this story to contemporary audiences.

JANUSZ KAMINSKI (director of photography): Clearly, due to my upbringing in Eastern Europe, there's a tremendous cultural difference between the movies I watched versus those that were popular in the United States. The sense of social realism was prevailing in Eastern Europe, whereas American cinema was always full of entertainment. Where I come from, musicals oftentimes were not viewed as serious cinema and were not fully embraced by viewers. Because I've lived here in America long enough, and I've studied film, I've learned to appreciate classic musicals such as *Singin' in the Rain* and *West Side Story*.

Steven Spielberg and screenwriter/executive producer Tony Kushner

A VISION FOR OUR TIMES

KRISTIE MACOSKO KRIEGER (producer): While *West Side Story* retains its message about the power of love and the danger of vilifying those who are different, it does take on new meaning today. We live in a deeply polarized world, and there's no denying that *West Side Story* has had a complicated history, especially among the Puerto Rican community. Steven, Tony, and our entire creative team understood from the beginning how important it was to have the Puerto Rican and Latinx communities see themselves represented on-screen. We all felt a responsibility—and recognized the incredible opportunity—to build a more accurate interpretation of this story, designed for our times.

KEVIN McCOLLUM (producer): I had produced *In the Heights* on Broadway, and I saw the need for more Latinx artists onstage. I felt the timing was right, and so in 2009 I did the revival of *West Side Story* on Broadway that Arthur Laurents directed. Arthur always said that the challenge with adapting *West Side Story* to the screen was the need for someone who not only could understand stage musicals, but also was a genius of film. And Arthur and I did speak about Steven Spielberg; coincidentally, it was at the time Steven was producing *Smash*, his musical series for television. I remember Steven came backstage after he saw the revival, and I told him then he would be a great director to revisit *West Side* as a movie. We chatted, and it seemed like this could really happen! I eventually pitched the idea to Emma Watts at what was 20th Century Fox, now part of Disney, and found out they had been trying to figure out how to remake it as well. Sometimes life is just about waiting until what you imagine actually happens.

West Side Story is such a classic that it deserved the prism of today and the portal of our time. It was important for us to honor the social and political climate of mid-century New York while also highlighting the relevance of this timeless story for modern audiences.

ALEXANDER BERNSTEIN (son of Leonard Bernstein): My father would have been pleased that Steven Spielberg is directing *West Side Story*, because he loved *Close Encounters of the Third Kind*. We saw it together, and I remember him being blown away by that film. He thought it was so brilliant and loved the idea of music being the language that humans and aliens used to communicate.

DAVID SAINT (literary executor, Arthur Laurents's estate): Arthur directed a new version of the Broadway show in 2008–09 and added Spanish for some of the dialogue and songs, written by Lin-Manuel Miranda. And if Arthur were alive today, I know he would have

Top
Protest scenes highlight the timeliness and urgency of *West Side Story*.

Above
Producer Kevin McCollum

Opposite
Steven Spielberg on the set for "Prologue"

loved this new film version, because it's such an honest retelling of the story.

KRISTIE MACOSKO KRIEGER: Tony Kushner is a longtime friend and trusted collaborator. What made Tony perfect for this particular project is his sheer brilliance as a playwright, and as a screenwriter—few can work and live in both worlds, but that's what, and *who*, *West Side Story* needed. Steven and I couldn't think of anyone better suited to translate the stage script for the big screen, while also preserving the elements that make seeing it as a live production so memorable. Tony brought a fresh perspective and literally breathed new life into these characters. Steven and Tony also both share a deep love and appreciation for this story, so their collaboration was grounded first and foremost in their respect for it and determination to do it justice. There's a powerful synchronicity between them that's rare to find, and their collaboration on *West Side Story* has recentered the narrative, illuminated the complicated themes, and underlined the historical context at the root of the conflict between the Sharks and the Jets.

TONY KUSHNER (screenwriter/ executive producer): My parents were both classical musicians—my father, a clarinetist and a conductor; my mother

a bassoonist—and they were of Leonard Bernstein's generation. He was very much a hero of theirs. I have a photo of my mother in some pub at Tanglewood; she's in a group of young musicians listening to Bernstein playing the piano and singing. I had a kids' book he'd written, an introduction to the orchestra. We watched his kids' concerts on TV, my parents listened to Bernstein's recordings of Mahler, of his own symphonies—and I was obsessed with the original cast album of *West Side Story*. I was only four when the film came out, so I'm not sure when I first saw it, probably in college. It's a great film, immensely influential, and I loved it a lot. My husband, Mark, and I watched it together when we started dating, and we were both crying by the end. I saw it onstage for the first time in Arthur Laurents's revival. There's no other musical quite like it; it's inarguably among the best ever written. *West Side Story* and then *Gypsy* redefined the form as much as Rogers and Hammerstein had redefined it a generation before.

I knew that Steven's mother was a pianist and he'd played the clarinet since he was a kid, and I knew he loved musicals. After we made *Lincoln*, he told me that he wanted to make a film of *West Side Story*, and he asked me to do the screenplay. I was really intrigued by his interest in taking it on, amazed as I often am by his chutzpah, his appetite for risk. And I was moved by how many of our current

struggles Steven felt could be explored in this sixty-year-old masterpiece—I guess moved and troubled, in a good way, because the racism, the xenophobia, the legacies of colonialism, the effects of poverty, the evils that catalyzed the creation of the musical, are still very much with us. Steven felt the time was right to take a new look at *West Side Story*, and he's always been remarkably attuned to the zeitgeist. As we talked, we both came to believe that, proceeding from our shared love and respect for this musical, we could find new and exciting things to try, new ways of bringing this story and this score to the screen.

STEVEN SPIELBERG: I wanted to explore the characters much more deeply and to give them reasons for being who they are. Tony Kushner has really provided depth, motivation, and stronger interplay among the characters, and made them more relatable.

Tony called me early on and told me that his husband, Mark Harris, had had a great idea: "What would you think if Doc is deceased? We still have Doc's Drugstore, but his widow, a Puerto Rican woman, is the proprietor, and we ask Rita Moreno to play her." And I said, "What a good idea!" And that began our conversation with Rita Moreno. Rita got so involved in the production, not just as an actor playing Doc's widow, Valentina, but also as our executive producer. She has a completely unique perspective, one that bridges the generations between movies, and makes a living connection between the first film and ours.

JUSTIN PECK (choreographer):

Jerome Robbins was one of the founding choreographers of New York City Ballet, which is the company that I call home as resident choreographer. I first came to New York to attend the School of American Ballet. That's where I was first exposed to the vast repertoire of Jerome Robbins. As a student, I would attend performances at New York City Ballet almost nightly, where many of Robbins's works were on display. I became enamored with his musicality,

style, and storytelling through dance. He was a real American choreographer, and his interest in American narratives was so apparent in all of his work. I would go to watch his ballets as often as I could.

Some favorites were his *Glass Pieces*, *The Cage*, *Fancy Free*, and *N.Y. Export: Op. Jazz*. But nothing was better than seeing New York City Ballet dance his *West Side Story Suite*. I had been inspired by the original film growing up, but seeing the dances performed live onstage was eye-opening. Incidentally, when I joined New York City Ballet as a professional dancer, the first lead role I ever performed was Bernardo in *West Side Story Suite*. I danced the part consistently

from the ages of nineteen to thirty-one, and the original choreography became second nature. I felt like with many of Jerome Robbins's works, I was able to learn from them from both observing them on the exterior as well as feeling them as a dancer from the inside out. When I started to make choreographic work of my own at the age of twenty, there is no doubt that I pulled from his influence and inspiration. In a way, this entire experience was like a very long runway preparation and study for taking on the choreography for the film. It allowed Robbins's pulse to remain active but not forced, all while giving me the permission and platform to make the choreography of the film my own.

JEANINE TESORI (supervising vocal producer): I got involved with *West Side Story* through Tony Kushner. The most important question I asked myself was, *Why now?* And it occurred to me that while the first *West Side Story* movie was revolutionary, revisiting it today, with what the camera can do, made sense. What Steven is doing through his directing, and what Justin is doing through the choreography, is bringing the audience right into the story, on a very intimate and immersive level. It's an incredible experience.

Top
"America"! David Alvarez (Bernardo), Steven Spielberg, and Ariana DeBose (Anita) discuss a sequence from "America."

Bottom
From left: Steven Spielberg, stunt coordinator Mark Fichera, production assistant Clay Lerner, second assistant director Josh Muzaffer, Harrison Coll (Numbers), Sean Harrison Jones (Action), script supervisor Jessica Lichtner, choreographer Justin Peck, Ansel Elgort (Tony), and Mike Faist (Riff) watching video playback of "Cool"

STEVEN SPIELBERG: This is *Romeo and Juliet*, but it's also a very relevant allegory for what's happening along our borders and for the systems in this country that reject anyone who isn't white. That's a big part of our story. The characters say and do things in our *West Side Story* they didn't say or do onstage or in the 1961 film, and much of that difference came from our determination to explore the story, its historical context, and what the young people of Lincoln Square and San Juan Hill were really like—the Sharks and the Jets. The Puerto Rican community that's involved in *West Side Story* existed at that time mainly between West Sixty-Fourth and West Seventy-Second Streets. There's a rich and important history of that community which we wanted to incorporate in our version of the musical. In some ways this has resulted in what some might consider to be a more realistic or even darker version of *West Side Story*.

JUSTIN PECK: Our script took many of the numbers and put them into different context; it was impossible to use the original choreography as it was, and so the Robbins estate and I mutually decided to feel this out. I spent two weeks in the studio working on "America" and "Cool." Steven would come in, film on his iPhone, and put rough edits together. At the end of those two weeks, the Robbins estate came in to view the work. We spoke about the approach, the choreography, the movement. Steven gave a very passionate speech about what the film meant to him and why he wanted to make it. Then we showed them the rehearsal. A day or two later they gave us approval. From that point, it was full speed ahead.

MATTHEW SULLIVAN (executive music producer/music supervisor): I worked with Justin Peck and Jeanine Tesori on the tempo, the arrangements of the songs in preproduction. We had storyboards, and as we were figuring out a song with the actors, Steven would do a lot of his own shooting on his iPhone, and we would then compare the footage with the storyboards and sometimes make changes. Ultimately, the storyboards were a really helpful tool on the set for everyone to understand what was inside Steven's head.

STEVEN SPIELBERG: This is probably one of the most intimidating projects I've ever taken on. It's really fun when you make a little movie and years later people say, "Hey, he or she made a masterpiece." But it's very intimidating—and a little crazy—to take a masterpiece of theater which has already been turned into a masterpiece of cinema and try to do it through your different eyes and a different sensibility. You have to demand of yourself, over and over again, justification for treading on what feels like sacred ground. We all did that, the riskiness of this enterprise was not lost on any of us. But everyone involved entered this project with tremendous love and

respect, bordering on reverence, for the show and obviously for its legendary creators. But we also knew we had to make a movie for our times and make it with a contemporary understanding and with contemporary values that we subscribe to.

I think great stories should be told again and again. I love the original film made by Robert Wise, who was a friend of mine, as is Walter Mirisch, who produced it through the Mirisch Company. And Walter has told me all kinds of great stories about the making of the picture. I assured Walter and Rita Moreno, both *West Side Story* veterans, that I didn't want to make this movie to fix what was never in any sense broken; I wanted to make my version, the same *and* distinctly different, recognizably *West Side Story* but also something new.

ADAM STOCKHAUSEN (production designer): The first question was about approach: if this was to be a film shot on locations on the streets of New York, or in a studio on soundstages. Steven's very first direction to me was to get the story outside and make it feel real. That's a pretty tall order, given that we had this first discussion in 2016 and we all know what New York's West Side looks like today.

We started to think about other areas in New York, or other cities that could stand for New York, 1957. San Juan Hill, where the story takes place, was west of Broadway around Sixty-Fourth Street up to around Seventy-

First Street. It's essentially the site where Lincoln Center stands now. It was considered a slum area and then was taken by the city to be leveled, in order to build Lincoln Center. We know what every single building looked like then and basically combed through every neighborhood to find something that could match up. The East Village had the right fire escapes, but the streets were too different. We looked up into Harlem, across the river into the Bronx, and then to New Jersey. We went as far as Philadelphia. We were looking not only for the right architectural elements but also for the ability to close streets. The dance sequences required us to fully close streets for hours, so we needed to be in places where that would be possible.

ROBERT STRIEM (supervising location manager): Once we found the locations, we had to do an extensive amount of set dressing, construction at the street levels—remove modern-day signs, lights, air conditioners, and whatever couldn't be achieved through visual effects.

West Side Story is a film about community in New York, and Steven Spielberg's approach to making the film has reflected the same spirit. We took a community approach. We didn't want to invade neighborhoods and take over; we're renting space from schools and churches and donating to athletic teams. We're doing things that enable the film to be

Top and Bottom
Concept art by Alexios Chrysikos

made, while also sharing that benefit with the community at large. We've done casting of background artists in the local communities in which we've shot to get local members to be in the movie. We're involving the tenants and landlords. The idea is for everyone to be included. But definitely, the word "community" has been our running theme.

KRISTIE MACOSKO KRIEGER: New York City is another character in *West Side Story*; it was essential to all of us that we capture its energy on film, simply because the narrative is so connected to the history of the

communities living in the neighborhood at the time. While I knew filming on the streets of New York would present a logistical challenge, we did all we could to bring that element as we organized the production; the combined efforts of our production designer, Adam Stockhausen; our executive producer/unit production manager, Daniel Lupi; our supervising location manager, Robert Striem; and unit production manager Carla Raij and her team worked tirelessly to transport us back to New York City, 1957. There's also Adam Somner, who is a frequent collaborator of Steven's and served as our first assistant director/executive

Concept art by Alexios Chrysikos

producer. He had arguably one of the most difficult jobs, setting up every scene, making sure our cast, background artists, and crew were where they needed to be so Steven could get his shots in a timely fashion. This production had many logistical challenges with many moving parts that included limiting disruption to local communities. We were also filming in the summer and were at the mercy of the weather, with daily life surrounding us. The entire team protected us from it all and maintained great respect and integrity, without ever compromising the storytelling and the rhythm of filming.

PAUL TAZEWELL (costume designer): Like Steven himself, I was very familiar with the film that was done in '61. That was a point of reference for both of us, and we decided that, as much as we love the film and what it was for then, we were very interested in redefining how the story was told and how it should have a more realistic and natural sense for today. As with the original Broadway musical, we chose to set it in 1957. It had to be reflective of that period and of those people as they actually were in New York City at the time, and to avoid the polished look of the original film.

After having that first meeting with Steven, I went directly to photographic research and immersed myself in the period. I then developed a color palette and costume sketches to communicate my ideas for the costumes and in turn presented those ideas for Steven to respond to. We went through the cast, character by character and group by group, figuring out what seemed to work for him and what didn't. It was important to create a difference between the two gangs. You have a gang of Caucasian teenagers against a gang of Puerto Rican and Latinx teenagers, and my task was, "How do I best achieve the differences between these two groups while supporting who they are as characters." For the Caucasian community, I was drawn toward the tones of cool blues and greens, teals and gray, which married well against the vast array of angular concrete buildings, sidewalks, and streets. The Latinx community contrasted with warm tones in golds, reds, and oranges; reflective of vivacity and aspiration in their color palette.

With the exception of "Dance at the Gym," the Jets are mired in the grime from the rubble that their neighborhood has become through urban renewal. With Tony, I cleaned him up from his past ties to his childhood gang environment. He is now working for Valentina, his surrogate parent, and he has developed a more optimistic view of changing his life. I wanted to make sure that this was clear from the first time we see him.

PATRICIA DELGADO (associate choreographer): I'm first-generation Cuban American. My family, my mom and dad, came to the United States in the sixties from different parts of Cuba, fleeing Castro's revolution. I can relate firsthand to that idea of displacement and to the complexities of appreciating America for the opportunities that it provides while not being able to be in your homeland, with your people. It was extraordinary to be connected to my Cuban roots on this project by having this opportunity to be surrounded by so many young, passionate, talented Latin people.

STEVEN SPIELBERG: The current concern with authenticity is complicated. It's a meeting point of so many issues, all of them related but still significant in their differences, concerns as various as discriminatory hiring patterns and practices, historical and cultural representational accuracy, ownership of one's identity and communal histories, appropriation and misappropriation, the assumptions of privilege, and even questions artists always need to ask themselves—the very real need people have to see themselves represented in art, about imagining lives and times other than one's own, about how real or unreal art should or shouldn't be. Complicated, like I said. *West Side Story* is a musical that's of its time and also about its time. But as soon as people start singing and dancing instead of talking, we think our audiences will get that this isn't intended as a documentary. That said, we took our responsibility very seriously to show a representation of the Puerto Rican community that Puerto Ricans will recognize and feel good about. We did extensive research, we consulted with Puerto Rican historians like Professor Virginia Sanchez-Korrol, we conducted seminars for ourselves and for the cast, we had two full-time Puerto Rican dialect coaches on set, working with the cast, and a number of people, including cast members, reviewing all the Spanish dialogue in the script to make sure we got it right. Every single prop, costumes, picket signs, street signs, wall mottos, the exact shade of color for the flag—we wanted to be authentic, and also I have to say everyone involved learned a lot, and that was a joy.

TONY KUSHNER: The story is both big and political and also intimate; at its heart it's as private and personal as can be, two young people who fall fiercely in love, but the love that blossoms between them is murdered by the big political world surrounding them. The story is a warning: Racism and nativism and poverty are democracy's antitheses, and if not resisted and rejected, they will atomize the bonds that hold us together as a society. Love, as they say, is the answer, love can transform the world, it can transform malevolent reality, but love doesn't conquer all, or at least not all threats in the immediate moment. In a context of hatred, love is in danger. And that is tragic, that's the tragedy of *West Side Story.*

JANUSZ KAMINSKI (director of photography): If we talk about this particular

Ariana DeBose (Anita) co-key makeup artist Mandy Bisesti, and costume designer Paul Tazewell

movie and the ways it differs from the original movie, the first thing to point out is the camera movement. When Robert Wise made his movie, at that point in film history, generally, the camera was rather static. In that first screen version of *West Side Story*, the choreography was beautiful, but it doesn't feel entirely motivated by the camera—or camera moves. We needed to do something different without reinventing the genre. So, we still have people dancing, people singing and performing in very beautiful, colorful costumes. Yet, from the standpoint of cinematography, it has a modern interpretation, and the modern aspect comes from how active the camera becomes. Today, the equipment is lighter; it allows us to move with the actors, which was much more challenging back in the late fifties.

The look of the original movie was bright— very colorful, and glossy. We embraced that aspect, but what we didn't like was the sterile aspect of the frame. The streets were too clean, there was no dirt. . . . It didn't feel realistic. It's very hard to make a musical feel gritty and real, because people are singing and that in itself is not true to life. We want the audience to feel enticed by the story, entertained by the dancing, moved by the lyrics, but on top of it, we want to really make it beautiful and a little bit more authentic. You feel the grit and the dirt of the street, and we created this environment by filming on location.

We shot the movie on film, as opposed to going digital. The technical aspect of shooting on film, versus digital files, brings you an element of reality and fits the particular period. Since it takes place in the fifties, film was really the only way to do it. Steven and I like film over digital. We like the discipline of it. Having only twelve or thirteen minutes of film per reel, having to say, "Cut and reset," reslating the clapboard, is good for everyone. Particularly in this movie, it was helpful for the dancers, because it gave them a little break. It fed the whole process.

In general, I feel that film still has a greater advantage over digital technology. When you're doing a contemporary movie that takes place on streets at night, digital has its place. Clearly there are amazing cinematographers who embrace the digital medium, and they can be at peace because there are no surprises; you can see the result right away. With film, there's still that aspect of anticipation, because you have to have it processed in the lab before you can see anything. I like that excitement; I like being nervous. It makes me anxious and it keeps me on my toes. There's that magical thing when the film is being exposed and the chemical process takes place. Sometimes, it doesn't come out right. And that's when you can embrace the technology, knowing that by digitizing the film negative you can manipulate it digitally and improve the image.

Opposite
From left: Ariana DeBose (Anita), Ilda Mason (Luz), and Ana Isabelle (Rosalía) filming "America" on the streets of New York

CREATING CHARACTERS

STEVEN SPIELBERG (director/producer): Rachel Zegler, our María, turned eighteen during preproduction. She had just graduated from high school as we started filming. Ariana DeBose, who starred in the original Broadway run of *Hamilton*, is playing Anita, and she's gotten the *Good Housekeeping* seal of approval from Rita Moreno herself. Our Rosalía, Ana Isabelle, is from Puerto Rico and is also a pop star there. They're all extraordinary—brilliant dancers, actors and singers. Same with the Jet girls, starting with Paloma Garcia-Lee, who plays Graziella.

Ansel Elgort as Tony is an incredible actor who can sing and dance. Mike Faist as Riff is amazing, fearless, intense, heartbreaking. David Alvarez, who plays Bernardo, is a fantastic, one-of-a-kind actor. I wanted a realistic Bernardo, a real tough guy who can lead his friends in defending their community, who has ambition and brains and wit, and David does all that and more. We decided to make the character of Chino upwardly mobile, educated, decent, loyal, the kind of great guy Bernardo would want his sister to marry. And we wanted the audience to feel that María and Chino could've been a brilliant couple—because so much of what makes *West Side Story* great is the longing it arouses in us for things to have worked out differently, which, in the story, they almost always could've. Again, with Josh Andrés Rivera, we found a Chino who really rivals Tony. He's a wonderful, deep, delightful actor.

And the Sharks and the Jets . . . God bless them all. We worked very hard to find the greatest ensemble imaginable, and with our genius casting director, Cindy

Tolan, we really did that. It took a year to cast this *West Side Story*. These actors were the best of the best, that's how they got cast. What we didn't know—you never know till the filming starts—is that we'd also assembled a cast that was phenomenally dedicated to the work. They were tireless, unstoppable. And I feel that all of their glorious work, souls, and talents are splendidly in evidence in the film.

KEVIN McCOLLUM (producer):
Broadway requires such a specific discipline. You have to do eight shows a week. You have to keep your body and mind in shape. You have to be an athlete. And that's why Hollywood is so excited to work with talent from the theater. It's been such a joyous experience for me, because I've worked already with so many cast members in the theater, and it's thrilling to witness them getting their big break on screen with this film. Everyone's here for the right reason. Everyone who is here wants to be here.

Above
Cindy Tolan, casting director

Opposite
Promotional boxing photo of Bernardo created for the film

CINDY TOLAN (casting director): My associate Nicholas Petrovich worked and collaborated with me very closely to cast this film. Steven Spielberg, his producer Kristie Macosko Krieger, Tony Kushner, Jeanine Tesori, Justin Peck and his team (Patricia Delgado and Craig Salstein) were always with us during open calls. We were all present at all times, and all had input and opinions. What's amazing about working with Steven and Kristie is that they give you everything you need to do your job. We knew that the only way we were going to do this film was if we could cast it appropriately.

We immediately put out social-media postings, announcing that we were casting Steven Spielberg's *West Side Story*, and it went viral. We started getting self-taped auditions from around the world and, in addition, went through the traditional channels of agents and massive open calls. We targeted New York, Florida, Puerto Rico, California, and all of Latin America. We hired satellite casting directors in those additional cities; they would film potential candidates and send it all to us. Every audition that came to our office was looked at. Anyone we thought would be appropriate, we would share with Steven. Based on his response, we would move on to next steps.

STEVEN SPIELBERG: Several of our *West Side Story* cast members are from Puerto Rico or are of Puertorriqueño heritage. The

Latinx community is represented in our cast, and also behind the camera. It would have been impossible, as well as unthinkable, for us to make a film of *West Side Story* without doing our best to gather a truly diverse cast and crew, and in countless ways, the diversity of the people who made this production gave it its form and substance.

RACHEL ZEGLER (María): I've lived in Clifton, New Jersey, my whole life. I started performing when I was twelve years old, and I played Shprintze in a local production of *Fiddler on the Roof.* I turned thirteen while I was in that show. It was an eye-opening experience, because I worked with a bunch of people who were my senior. Our cast ranged from ten to seventy-five years old. It really made me want to perform for the rest of my life. I kept auditioning for things and doing different shows, playing a variety of parts. I always wanted to do it on a professional scale and make it my job, make it my life. Part of me never thought it was realistic, and now it is. It's become my reality.

JEANINE TESORI (supervising vocal producer): Rachel and I have now known each other for more than a year. She came to us with a beautiful voice, and I have watched her evolve—she is so curious and has the ability to learn on the spot.

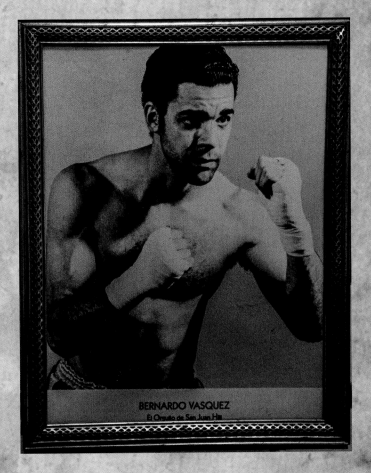

BERNARDO VASQUEZ
El Orgullo de San Juan Hill

When I first recorded with Rachel, she had never done a session before. That was the beauty of starting with a seventeen-year-old. She brought that openness; we would work and work, and I saw her come of age.

KRISTIE MACOSKO KRIEGER (producer): María is often thought of as a classic ingenue, but when you look beneath the surface of the text, she embarks on a personal journey as a young woman living in a new and uncertain place. She begins the film as an innocent optimist and grows into someone who knows what she wants and fights for it. It was clear that Rachel drew upon her own family's history of coming to America from Colombia, and brought a strength and sense of purpose to the role that stem from that personal inspiration.

ANSEL ELGORT (Tony): I grew up listening to Broadway soundtracks, and I first knew about *West Side Story* through the music. After I saw *Oklahoma* as a kid, I became obsessed with Broadway; my dad would burn me tons of Broadway CDs. *The King and I*, *A Chorus Line*, *Rent*, and *West Side Story* were among my favorites. My dad showed me the film by Robert Wise as well. He saw the original Broadway production with his brother when he was a kid; he still talks about it and said it was the most amazing thing he ever saw. I saw it on Broadway maybe ten years ago when they were doing it in Spanish and English. I even played Action in a summer camp production of *West Side Story*, so it was definitely part of my upbringing.

JULIO MONGE (dialect coach): The reality of the time when *West Side Story* first appeared was that there weren't that many Puerto Ricans trained as dancers/singers/actors. And even when I got to New York in the eighties, the demographic was still imbalanced; I was one of two or three Puerto Ricans in *Jerome Robbins' Broadway*, among a cast of seventy. I got used to that, but then I started seeing a change. It's amazing now to see this new production of *West Side Story* and to have so many Puerto Rican performers in it.

DAVID AVILÉS MORALES (Aníbal): I was born and raised in Puerto Rico. It's my island. My heart is there. I started dancing when I was a kid and fell in love with ballet and different styles of dance. When I was thirteen years old, my aunt gave me the movie *West Side Story* as a Christmas gift. From that moment on, I became obsessed with it. I grew up in a project back home, and none of my friends really knew about my dancing. I used to sneak out to my ballet classes. My family was aware, and even though they needed the money and would have wanted me to become a lawyer or a doctor, they were very supportive and really made it possible for me to be here today, making this film.

When I first met Steven, I just let him know, "I'm not a singer, I'm not an actor, I'm just a passionate dancer. I have a special love for my country, for my people, and for *West Side Story*. I basically started dancing because of it, and now I'm in it!" I always thought the actors in the first film were Puerto Ricans, and when I found out that wasn't the case [except for Rita Moreno], it broke my heart. It makes me even more proud to be Puerto Rican and to be part of the cast in this new version of *West Side Story*.

CINDY TOLAN: We were struggling to find the right Bernardo. We had options, but we weren't really landing on the person who could fulfill the role Steven was envisioning. And we just had one of those moments where we remembered David Alvarez as one of the Billys in the Broadway

Above
Thoughtful between takes: Rachel Zegler (María)

production of *Billy Elliot: The Musical*, which he had done when he was just a kid and had won a Tony Award for. David was off the grid as a performer, and we tracked him down and blasted his inbox through all the social media outlets. It took him two weeks to respond. When we got his self-audition, as soon as I saw it, I texted Kristie and said, "I think I found Bernardo." She and Steven watched it and instantly agreed David was a strong candidate for Bernardo.

DAVID ALVAREZ (Bernardo): I was born in Montréal, Canada, in 1994 to my Cuban parents, who had defected in '93. My dad was able to find a job in San Diego, California, and we spent five years there. My mom had put me in ballet because I used to get injured in school playing soccer, and that's where my love for

not just dance but anything art-related grew. I auditioned for ABT JKO's [American Ballet Theatre Jacqueline Kennedy Onassis's] American Ballet School and was offered a full scholarship to come to New York, and we moved there. My career took off with *Billy Elliot* on Broadway and *On the Town*. I then spent some time in the military; when I returned, I was ready to do something demanding and challenging. Somehow, I ended up doing *West Side Story* with Steven Spielberg, and it's been a beautiful experience; it's as if everything has led me up to this point.

The first time I heard about this movie was through my social media, from casting director Cindy Tolan. It seemed like a long shot, but Cindy suggested that I send something. . . . She asked that I do the "Quintet," and either that same day or the next one, I got a call back from

Cindy Tolan saying that Steven Spielberg saw the tape, that he loved it and wanted to see me. All of a sudden, this huge door opened up on new opportunities, new experiences, and moments of learning as well. When I met with Steven—I called him "Mr. Spielberg," trying to stay professional. And he said, "Oh, please don't call me Mr. Spielberg, call me Steven, because I'll be calling you Bernardo from now on." After that I started digging into the character and started figuring out how I wanted to bring this to life.

MIKE FAIST (Riff): I celebrated my ten-year anniversary of being in New York back in June 2019. I'm originally from Ohio. I moved to go to a conservatory program here in the city. I decided to drop out and was doing theater gigs here and there. I was in *Dear Evan Hansen* recently— Steven came to it, and we talked. I first auditioned for *West Side Story* in February 2018; I actually auditioned originally for Tony. I didn't hear anything back. They asked if I would come back in for Riff. November 2018 is when it solidified.

I'm primarily an actor. But I grew up taking dance classes and voice lessons. This is my first big movie, and when I first sat down with Steven, I told him the movies I grew up watching were *Singin' in the Rain*, *West Side Story*, and Indiana Jones. I told him, jokingly, I was bred and groomed to do this with him.

SEBASTIAN SERRA (Braulio): Braulio is one of Bernardo's best friends. If something

happens to Bernardo, Braulio takes over. I'm from Puerto Rico. And I knew, back home, some of the Sharks. Having this experience with people that you already know from your past is extraordinary. It made the filming process easier and more comfortable.

JOSH ANDRÉS RIVERA (Chino): I read for Bernardo in March 2019, while I was on the national tour with *Hamilton*. Seven months later, I went in for Bernardo and Chino, and I eventually got a call from my agent saying, "You booked it. You're Chino." I literally got off the phone, I processed it for a second, and then I just started crying.

JULIUS ANTHONY RUBIO (Quique): I live in New York City. I was originally born in Santo Domingo, in the Dominican Republic, but I was raised in Miami. I'm a firm believer that everything comes from the top, and Steven is very, very clear about taking care of everybody, and not just people in front of the camera, everybody behind the camera as well. And that's really what I keep bragging about to my friends and my family, that the environment, even if we're working on hostile material between the Sharks and the Jets, Steven made it seem like it was home since day one.

ANDREI CHAGAS (Jochi): I'm originally from Rio de Janeiro, Brazil. I started dancing ballet when I was eleven. I moved to Florida with the Miami City Ballet for a year. That's when I got to know Justin Peck, and I auditioned to do *Carousel* with him on Broadway. That led to this amazing production of *West Side Story*. Along with the other Sharks, I'm representing the people from Latin America who have been through the same struggle that this movie is depicting.

BEN COOK (Mouthpiece): When I went in for the audition at Gelsey Kirkland, the dance studio where we ended up doing our rehearsals, there was a massive line. It just strung around the entire block, and I said to myself, *Wow, that's a lot of people.* But I didn't panic. I was still very excited. And this ended up being the first of several auditions. Eventually, I was fortunate enough to get cast. I'm unbelievably grateful.

KEVIN CSOLAK (Diesel): I knew a bunch of people coming in for auditions, because for the past two years, I've been blessed to be in Broadway musicals, and a lot of the cast for this movie are Broadway performers. To come into this process and see so many familiar faces and a few close friends, like Ben Cook, who plays Mouthpiece, immediately created a really comfortable work environment.

RACHEL ZEGLER: *West Side Story* definitely was something that was around in my childhood, the music and the original film. And I remember my mom talking about Rita Moreno when I was a kid, and how incredible

Costume sketch of Anita by Miodrag Guberinic

she was for the Latin community. I played María when I was sixteen years old for a community theater, and about six months later the audition notice for this new film went out. I sat down with a horrendous haircut, and I sang "I Feel Pretty" in Spanish. . . . It was embarrassing, but they saw it. They emailed me about two weeks later, asking me to send in another tape singing "Somewhere" and to read some of the sides from Tony Kushner's incredible script. They liked it. Cindy Tolan asked me to come in person to record another audition in her office in Chelsea. I did that. Then my mom got a call from Cindy's office, saying that Steven wanted to meet me in person. They asked me to come out to Lincoln Center for a work session in the beginning

of June 2018. I got there, and it was Justin Peck and Patricia Delgado teaching a group of Marías and a group of Tonys this dance that never really made it into "Dance at the Gym." Suddenly, we heard barking, and this beautiful dog came up to me—it was Steven's. Then Steven himself came in and individually introduced himself to all of us. I just remember being speechless, yet grateful. I just kept thanking him for letting us be here and for even agreeing to see us. We also met Kate Capshaw, his wife—it was quite a moment.

We proceeded with a four-day work session at Lincoln Center, filled with singing, acting, and dancing in front of Steven, Tony Kushner, Jeanine Tesori, Patricia, Justin, Kate, and, of course, the dog. It was terrifying, because I was also studying for my finals at the same time. On the last day of the work session, we all went home. That night I got a call from Cindy, who told me I was moving on to the next round—a screen test at Steiner Studios. That's when I met Ansel.

ANSEL ELGORT: It was a no-brainer in terms of my wanting to do this film. I just had to earn it and get it. And I was in the middle of doing another movie when I had to start auditioning. I started working on "María," but I didn't quite nail the song. I sent in the recording anyway. Cindy, the casting director, kept saying to me she wasn't going to give those to Steven and to keep trying. I did. I kept working with my

Costume sketch of Riff by Shane Ballard

vocal coach, trying to get better and better, and luckily, I earned a screen test. When I came for it, everyone was there, Steven and his director of photography, Janusz Kaminski. Rachel was one of the Marías, and we tested together. There were other Marías and other Tonys there, as well, and tons of Anitas and Bernardos.

RACHEL ZEGLER: We did the balcony scene, which was beautiful. I remember Steven looking at Ansel and shaking his hand at the end of the day, saying, "You surprised me today." And I immediately thought, *He just booked it. He just got the part.*

ARIANA DeBOSE (Anita): *West Side Story* found me. I certainly was not looking for it. In fact, I remember when they made the big announcement that Steven Spielberg was going to make this film, I immediately thought, *That's one job I'll never get!* In my mind, I believed they'd want a very fancy pop star. And then Cindy Tolan had a conversation with my agent, and they asked me to come in. I did, reluctantly, and I kept telling myself I was wrong for this project. But to fully understand my attitude, I have to talk about my background. My mom is white; my father is Puerto Rican. I didn't have the good fortune to grow up with my father in my life, for various reasons. My mom raised me as a single parent. I remember growing up, people always asking me if I was adopted. Everyone assumed I was African American. I had to constantly search for who I was. I remember

taking those incredibly silly standardized tests where they ask you to claim an ethnicity. At one point I checked every single box until one of my teachers finally said to me, "Well, you only get to claim one." I replied, "I don't know how to do that, because I'm a little bit of everything." With that in mind, I was very scared to fully commit myself to this role—it meant that I would have to dive into a part of myself that I had grown a healthy amount of shame about. I don't speak Spanish, but once I committed to this part, it became a gift of acceptance about who I am. It also meant being accepted by the Latin and Hispanic communities, and more importantly by the Puerto Rican community. It's something I never thought I would ever find.

TONY KUSHNER (screenwriter/ executive producer): When Ariana auditioned, we asked her to sing some of "America." When she got to the lines "And the babies crying, / And the bullets flying," there were tears in her eyes; she got the horror of what she was singing and she made us see it. She's a great dramatic actress. She does nothing for effect—her power comes from the truth.

PALOMA GARCIA-LEE (Graziella): My mom was a Broadway performer and pretty much made a career out of doing *West Side Story* on many national and international tours. She is Hispanic and was a Shark. I played Graziella when I was fifteen years old at the North Carolina School of the Arts, with the original Jerome Robbins choreography. Getting

to do this role again, but on this scale, has been so meaningful and has brought me full circle.

TANAIRI SADE VAZQUEZ (Charita):
I felt very confident coming into the audition. I remember being a little girl and my parents showing me the movie and asking myself, who are those lucky women who get to dance and act in a movie? And now it's hitting me that I'm part of the history of *West Side Story*. My parents live in Puerto Rico, and I called them every day during filming, to share what this experience has been.

JENNIFER FLORENTINO (Montse):
I am so fortunate to have parents who were willing to sacrifice their homes and their lives to come to America, to have the opportunity to make a living here and create all these new opportunities. It's a perfect time for me and my family to be proud of being Latinos, and to experience this movie.

HARRISON COLL (Numbers): My parents were both in musical theater. My mom, Susan Hartley, was a singer, dancer, and actress on Broadway, and my dad, Richard Coll, started as a tap dancer on Broadway and later became a filmmaker. He was an avid follower of Jerome Robbins and knew every step of choreography from both the film and Broadway versions of *West Side Story*. He seemed like a Jet at heart. I've actually seen some of Robbins's archival

Costume sketch of Tony by Shane Ballard

audition notes from an audition that my dad attended for the show *Gypsy*. My dad went by "Ricky" back then—Robbins put a check mark, an "OK," and an A– for singing next to his name! But ever since I was a kid, I remember *West Side Story* music playing at home. Being part of Steven's *West Side Story* production connected me to my father, whom I'd recently lost to pancreatic cancer. He survived for eighteen months before succumbing to the disease—I will never forget how he battled it every day, determined to live like he'd always lived, with gusto and guts.

The entire process of this film from start to finish connected me to him. I remember getting the email about the audition and feeling like I needed to make sure my dad was by my side. So I brought a small vial of his ashes to keep in my back pocket. I'd auditioned many times for the stage, but this was my first film audition. I was nervous at first but also incredibly grounded and ready to give it everything I had. I knew my dad was watching over me, his strength radiating from my left back pocket. Amazingly, I was invited to be a Jet, and I know my dad had something to do with that.

JULIETTE FELICIANO (Cuca): From the start, I was very shy, being the tiniest one, and the youngest one among the Sharks women. But they really shook me out of it and were very supportive. It was definitely like becoming part of a family.

Tony (Ansel Elgort) serenading María

RICARDO A. ZAYAS (Chago): The film is similar to the story of my parents coming from Puerto Rico at a young age with my uncles, aunts, and my grandparents, and them looking for a different and better life—but they did not know what they were going to find. . . . They were just hopeful and determined people. Puerto Ricans in general are very proud, and this role has helped me tap into that pride. I feel like I have a lot of people besides my parents whose story we're telling here.

SKYE MATTOX (Maxie): When I moved to New York I was seventeen, and the 2009 Broadway revival was being cast; I auditioned

for it, and I ended up going on the international tour for it. I came back and did the revival here in the city for eight months, followed by the national tour. So *West Side Story* has been a big part of my career.

JONALYN SAXER (Rhonda): I really love the first movie, but this type of dancing always seemed unattainable to me. Part of me always thought, *Oh, I would never be able to do that.* And yet, I went to the audition and here I am!

DAVID GUZMAN (Tino): My brother, Jason, and I are identical twins, but we're not playing twins in the movie. Being twins, we were always on the same wavelength, and we auditioned together for *West Side Story*. It's the one show I've always wanted to be in, being Puerto Rican; it has such strong male energy as well as a balletic feeling.

JACOB GUZMAN (Junior): We grew up in Brockton, Massachusetts, and we started dancing when we were two years old at the Gold School; we've been dancing ever since. We moved to New York for our senior year of high school and joined the Broadway show *Newsies*, and our careers took off from there.

KYLE ALLEN (Balkan): I did sports, acrobatics, gymnastics for about six years. I did classical ballet for about five years and

then turned to acting in films and television four years ago, before this project came up. And it got me back into dance; I taught myself how to sing, and here we are.

YUREL ECHEZARRETA (Sebas): *West Side Story* was one of the first shows I ever did for theater, and it's amazing that I'm now trying to make the transition into movies through this new film version.

CARLOS SÁNCHEZ FALÚ (Pipo): This movie is the first time that I've been outside Puerto Rico. I'm now living here in New York City, and the guys became my family. They're the first people I encountered after I got the part. There's this sense of confidence between us; we can trust each other.

EDRIZ E. ROSA PÉREZ (Jacinta): *West Side Story* has changed my life in so many ways. It's just brought so much confidence in me. If Steven Spielberg picked me, it's because I have something. And being next to so many talented people has been a big boost.

RICKY UBEDA (Flaco): I'm from Cuba, and *West Side Story* is extremely relevant to today's political climate and just everything that's happening in the world today. It was important to bring an authentic Latin feel to the Sharks. I feel honored to be able to have a small part with all these guys in representing the Hispanic community.

ILDA MASON (Luz): I did not know *West Side Story* growing up in Panama. I moved to New York six years ago. It was not until I came to study musical theater that I became familiar with the story. Since then I have been in two productions of *West Side Story*, and this one is my third. I have fallen in love with it, because it is my story as well, even though I'm not Puerto Rican. As an immigrant, I look at the sadness of what these characters lived through compared to what is happening in this country today—you can see the similarities.

ARIANA DeBOSE: Even during the audition process, Steven was very clear on who the character of Anita was. She's strong; she's fiery. She deeply loves life. It's been hard to come as far as she has. Steven said that the road for her from Puerto Rico to New York was very tumultuous. She wears that, but it does not completely define her. I've tried to reference all of that throughout production. After I got the role, Steven said, "You are her, and she is you. And you don't really have to try, I just want you *to be*, and she'll come out." And he was right. I'm typically the consummate planner. I work very hard. I study; I beat a scene on paper to an inch of its life. But there came a point in this process where I no longer had to do that.

Costume sketches of Rhonda and Anita by Miodrag Guberinic

RACHEL ZEGLER: I went in for a chemistry reading with Ansel in January 2019. And it was like greeting an old friend. I had some great conversations and really hung out with Steven and Ansel all day. It was a very chill, calm environment. Steven offered me the role in person that day. He told Ansel and me to leave the room. They brought my mom in and called us back in. Steven walked up and said, "I want to let you know that you've gotten the part of María." And I screamed "Holy shit!" to his face. And he gave me this big hug.

TONY KUSHNER: While I was working on the screenplay, I had complicated backstories for the characters in my head and my notebook, but in a musical with songs and dancing and a big cast of characters there isn't room for much of that kind of information. Rachel asked me for more background about María, and then David and Mike Faist called, and then Rita Moreno, so I started writing detailed biographies, the characters' lives before the musical's story begins, where they were born, where they live now in 1957, what they do for a living, their families, politics, religious beliefs, turning points in their lives. I wanted the cast to be aware of relevant histories of the US and Puerto Rico, the immigrants who had settled in the Lincoln Square area, the Puerto Rican

From top: John Michael Fiumara (Big Deal) and Adriana Pierce (Natalie); Julius Anthony Rubio (Quique) and Maria Alexis Rodriguez (Isa); Mike Faist (Riff) and Paloma Garcia-Lee (Graziella)

diaspora neighborhood of San Juan Hill, the mass evacuation and demolition of the entire area to make way for Lincoln Center. It was fun and it was exhausting.

JESS LePROTTO (A-Rab): From Tony Kushner's backstory, A-Rab got his name because of his "outlier status." As a Jet, he is true to the core, but his intense drive and volatile attitude make him a thorny addition to the gang. His original name is Gabriel, and he comes from a Sicilian background. For me, as A-Rab, it was essential to show that he was unique and a true individual.

KEVIN CSOLAK: Diesel is obsessed with cars, but his obsession got him in some big trouble. He tried to steal a car from an auto shop, and three workers there practically beat him senseless. He was unconscious as Riff and Ice came out of nowhere and saved him before the guys finished the job. From then on, Diesel owed Riff and the gang his life. He got introduced into the Jets, and Riff named him Diesel due to his first love: cars.

KYLE COFFMAN (Ice): Ice is my name because I'm cool as ice. I've got ice in my veins. I never let anything rattle me. And my real name is Isidor, and it was Riff who nicknamed me Ice. The Jets are not allowed to call me Isidor or Izzy. Just Ice.

PALOMA GARCIA-LEE: In Tony Kushner's backstory, Graziella and Tony used to date before he went to prison. She is now dating Riff, but you see a

From top: David Avilés Morales (Aníbal) and Edriz E. Rosa Pérez (Jacinta); Yurel Echezarreta (Sebas) and Isabella Ward (Tere); Ben Cook (Mouthpiece) and Maddie Ziegler (Velma)

few moments in the film where she still has a lot of love for Tony. . . . When he falls in love with María, you can feel her pain. It's really tragic, because she loses both of them. I thank Tony Kushner for the depth of character he gave to this woman.

VIRGINIA SÁNCHEZ KORROL (consultant/ historian): Rita Moreno was the only Puerto Rican actress in the first movie, and our community was thrilled. And then she won the Oscar! It was such an amazing accomplishment for this young Puerto Rican girl, who, in a sense, represented our people. I had been a fan of hers since her first movie, and I favored films with a Latino theme, especially with Latinas in the cast. Olga San Juan, who was another Puerto Rican actress working at the time, actually came from my childhood neighborhood in the Bronx.

TONY KUSHNER: Valentina's backstory is twenty-five pages long. It's like a little novel, starting with her early life in Puerto Rico, and it includes how Tony came to live in the basement of her drugstore. It spans the first half of the twentieth century. While I was writing it, I fantasized that I was watching an epic miniseries starring Rita Moreno.

RITA MORENO (Valentina): When I first heard about this new film, I was worried, because initially I had nothing to do with it. And then about three or four months after it was announced, my agent said, "Steven Spielberg wants to talk to you." He called me, and he told me how much he appreciated my performance in the

From top: Kyle Allen (Balkan) and Leigh-Ann Esty (Gussie); Kellie Drobnick (Mamie) and Kevin Csolak (Diesel); Carlos Sánchez Falú (Pipo) and Gabriela M. Soto (Conchi)

original movie, and how he'd love to have me as executive producer and in the film, playing the part of a new character named Valentina, the widow of Doc, who ran the candy store. I was just astonished; I asked for the script by Tony Kushner, read it, and thought it was brilliant. I was afraid Valentina would be a small part, but it's not a cameo. It's a real honest-to-God part, and she runs the drugstore now, by herself, and she's friendly with Tony. She's helping him out, and they have this wonderful relationship.

KRISTIE MACOSKO KRIEGER: Twenty members of the cast—including Rita Moreno—are Puerto Rican or are of Puerto Rican descent. Rita Moreno not only has this rich history with *West Side Story*, but also grew up in New York City around the time the film is set. Steven and Tony have done an immense amount of research about the Nuyorican community in 1957 and looked up to Rita to answer many of the questions they had.

Her perspective was invaluable. It was a huge asset to have her present to inform our young actors on the emotions they might be feeling at different moments of the story.

JENNIFER FLORENTINO: I'm from the Dominican Republic; a little place called Habo de la Hadeta.

This film is a chance for me to represent a culture, its strength and also the vulnerability within a period where women were trying to have a voice and stand up for themselves. They were looking to have a sense of equality; they were working and also trying to take care of their children or their sisters and brothers, while trying to make money. So when I think about being a Shark woman, I have to be responsible and show a certain amount of strength. I feel very fortunate to be an example for young girls out there, make them see our history, and that everything is possible.

JEANETTE DELGADO (Ili): My sister Patricia is the associate choreographer and is married to Justin Peck. I just happened to be in New York when they were putting together a workshop to show Steven Spielberg what Justin was thinking about for the dance movements. And so, by luck, he asked me to help and play Anita for the workshop. That was before the part was cast. At the end of it, Steven said he wanted me to be in the film—that's how I ended up as a Shark woman!

EZRA MENAS (Anybodys): It was very cool to hear that the part had grown from this tomboy sidekick character over time. I have always questioned the gender of Anybodys. It felt like, to me, it was a trans character. I'm a nonbinary trans person, so I'm always looking for representation of myself or my community in musical theater, so this role was perfect.

Once I got the part, in creating the look for Anybodys, each department really captured the essence of this person. They would ask me how I felt about certain things, and it was a gift to be able to contribute to the overall approach. Tony Kushner generously wrote a character background for each of us, with the whole plot intertwined. It was stunning to read. We witness Anybodys being raised and socialized as a young girl; and many times throughout the story Anybodys self-describes as a boy. They demand that they are seen in their true identity. I learned from Tony's thorough backstory that Anybodys comes from a broken home, with an alcoholic father, and began work at a shipyard from a very young age. We meet Anybodys after their being disowned, in search of a home, sleeping on the streets, and following the Jets closely. We see this lost soul, hoping to join this gang of brothers, not only to be accepted into a family unit, but also to be accepted for who they are as a person and in their authentic identity.

PATRICK HIGGINS (Baby John): I'm a junior in high school; I'm sixteen—the youngest of the Jets and the youngest in the cast. Ever since the very first open call, I completely submerged myself in *West Side Story*. I've watched a lot of movie musicals, and most of them are just all happy fun, everything's great, but *West Side Story* really brought real issues to the forefront: race and differences between people, as well as primal animosity and anger.

TALIA RYDER (Tessa): I met Patrick Higgins, who would eventually be my dance partner, the day of my final callback. When we were all getting paired at the callback, I was hoping to be paired with him, because he seemed to be the only other teenager in the room. Even though the combination was difficult, Patrick and I were open with each other and asked a lot of questions, which made the process really enjoyable. I learned that we were both in high school and both had a love for YouTube. When we weren't dancing, we were laughing. We always had a great time.

JOHN MICHAEL FIUMARA (Big Deal): There was an audition in New York City, but I actually couldn't go to that because I was living in Chicago doing *Hamilton*. So, I ended up using a "personal day off" and went to Los Angeles and auditioned. And then there were callbacks in New York. And more callbacks! It was quite a process.

SEAN HARRISON JONES (Action):

My sister Felicia passed away when I was three. She loved to dance. When my brothers and I went to what would have been her final dance recital that year, people asked us if we were going to start dancing, and we replied, "Yes." It just picked up from there. She's the reason I dance.

CINDY TOLAN: When we were pulling together the Jets and Sharks, and collectively creating who they would be, it became very clear that they would all come from completely different backgrounds and would all have different stories.

There were so many heartbreaks. For every person cast, there are at least five or six other actors who are equally gifted, equally talented, who didn't ultimately get cast. We could have cast this movie three times over. For various reasons, this is the group that we have in the movie, and they are spectacular. But there are so many amazing people out there that I remember, will remember, and will be bringing in for future roles.

Opposite
Ezra Menas (Anybodys) and Steven Spielberg

Right
Costume sketches of a trio of Jets and Chino by Shane Ballard

REHEARSALS

KRISTIE MACOSKO KRIEGER (producer): We announced our principal cast in January 2019 and began rehearsals in April. The first day of rehearsals was also the day we announced our full cast of Sharks and Jets; it felt like the first day of school.

STEVEN SPIELBERG (director/producer): In a way, we were in production on this film for about five months before we started shooting. From the tireless work of Kristie Macosko Krieger and also Adam Somner, to the rehearsals, during which I started framing and storyboarding the song and dance numbers; the choreography with Justin Peck; the music; the orchestration; Jeanine Tesori's work getting everybody primed and ready to sing these songs as great as our cast could ever sing them.

BEN COOK (Mouthpiece): We had a read-through of the script, from start to finish; we read and sang through the entire show, and it was unbelievable.

KRISTIE MACOSKO KRIEGER: Because our cast is so young and lives in a world very different from the one portrayed in the film, we felt it was important to educate them about the historical and social context in which their characters lived. We set up panel discussions with cultural experts and people who lived in the San Juan Hill neighborhood at the time the story is set. These men and women saw the changes the neighborhood underwent and were able to offer the cast a window into what life was like back then. Many Puerto Rican migrants joined gangs out of sheer necessity and as a form of protection, and that was something we wanted to

bring to the forefront of the film. It was exciting to see our cast so engaged and eager to flesh out a realistic picture of who their characters were.

VIRGINIA SÁNCHEZ KORROL (historical consultant): Here you have a story about two gangs at war. They're males. This is a male-dominated film. At that moment of crisis, what are the women doing? I thought we should have a discussion session just for the women in the cast. Even though the role of women would become very important in the years following the film's time frame, the most important life event for a woman at that particular moment was to marry and have children. That was paramount in their lives. And marriage was what women wanted, even if they had a college education and career options. Still, in the coming decade the feminist movement would influence many women to break out of the role of domesticity. So we had a long discussion regarding women's roles in *West Side Story*. I commented, "You're really bright, you know exactly what you want. You know how to get it. But you are going to be even brighter in a couple of years."

DAVID ALVAREZ (Bernardo): I read a lot about the Mau Maus gang and the sixties. I started to read *War Against All Puerto Ricans* [by Nelson Antonio Denis], which is a very insightful book on everything the community has gone through, from one hundred years ago to the present day, and everything they continue to go through. I was trying to first figure out

the background and story behind Bernardo and what made him the person he ultimately is today.

RACHEL ZEGLER (María): About a month after I got cast, we went into training my voice with my coach, Joan Lader, as well as training for my posture and dialect. I was going in for fittings, hair appointments, makeup, and all these things.

My family on my mom's side is from Barranquilla, Colombia. My dad is Polish American. I grew up in an English-speaking home, but the Spanish language was spoken around my house, and I learned it in school. As I stepped into the role of María, it was very important to me that I familiarize myself even further with the language.

ANSEL ELGORT (Tony): The rehearsals were really important because we got a chance to all meet and become the Jets, and for Mike [Faist] and me to become best friends, and for Rachel and me to start to warm up to each other. Behind the scenes, the Jets and the Sharks didn't hate each other; we couldn't help it—we were all so friendly. We got to do ballet every day, which was essential leading up to filming. We intensely rehearsed all those dance numbers. When we got there on the day, we knew the dance totally impulsively.

RACHEL ZEGLER: Gelsey Kirkland Dance Studio functioned like a factory. Once rehearsals began, we weren't apart from that day on. We would warm up at the barre together as a group in the morning. It was the time to breathe as a community and just welcome the day. We would then dive into work. Our second assistant director for that phase, Billy Brennan, would come in and say, "Sharks are going to go into this room, and Jets are going to be here. María and Tony are doing a cha-cha rehearsal." And we just didn't stop moving the whole day. I would go from cha-cha with Ansel, to vocals for "I Feel Pretty," to dialect while trying to fit in some tutoring, because I was still seventeen.

PATRICIA DELGADO (associate choreographer): Sometimes I would create a playlist of Latin music for our ballet warm-ups, to help bond the Sharks and connect to our roots. Most days, however, we would all warm up together, Jets and Sharks, and that was an incredibly humbling, bonding, and inspiring experience for everyone. No matter our backgrounds, culturally or physically, we would start at the barre with ballet and watch one another dance, and everyone supported each other. Some people were completely out of their comfort zones. Some had never even taken ballet. To me it was somewhat spiritual, a commitment to ourselves and each other and

Previous spread
Ezra Menas (Anybodys), Ben Cook (Mouthpiece), Sean Harrison Jones (Action), Mike Faist (Riff), Patrick Higgins (Baby John), Ansel Elgort (Tony), Rachel Zegler (María), David Alvarez (Bernardo), Julius Anthony Rubio (Quique), Ricardo A. Zayas (Chago), Josh Andres Rivera (Chino), Sebastian Serra (Braulio), Carlos Sanchez Falú (Pipo)

Right
Costume sketches of Tony by Shane Ballard

the story we were telling! Everyone committing to being the best version of ourselves.

CRAIG SALSTEIN (associate choreographer): Basically, we broke the rehearsals up into four weeks to design and then eight weeks to mount the numbers as an ensemble. We had a smaller group in the first four weeks, and then we had the entire group in the remaining eight weeks. The most important thing for me was to facilitate an environment in which Justin could choreograph, drill, and present. The environment of the rehearsals, however, was not the conditions we eventually performed in for the film. It was a studio with the lights on, no costume, and it was important for me to remind the artists they needed to put into their minds that they would have outside elements to contend with once we got to set.

ARIANA DeBOSE (Anita): Rita Moreno came in and spoke to us all, told stories about Jerry Robbins, the experience of the original film, and working with George Chakiris. . . . And then she stopped and she said, "Wait. . . . Where is the girl playing Anita?" Everyone turned and looked at me, and then there was like a *whoo-hoo, clap-clap-clap*. I felt awkward, so I stood up. And Rita went, "You and me got some talking to do." I have to be honest, this wasn't the way I wanted to be introduced to her. But I found her during our lunch break and just said, "Hi. I would like to know whatever it is you would like to tell me. And I'm thoroughly terrified of doing this but I'm very excited to do it with you." And she replied, "Oh, honey, it's a lot." I knew she got it, and we just sat, had a lovely lunch, and talked as women. It was very simple and lovely. Rita Moreno is the epitome of grace, and, yes, she is hilarious, and she is Old Hollywood glam. She's a big personality. Yet underneath all of that she's still very much human, and she sees people. But, with all that aside, it was still tough. It is hard to make yourself vulnerable to the world's judgment of your interpretation of an iconic work. What she did with that character was iconic. With the help of Steven and of the entire creative team, especially Tony Kushner, I've been able to find something really new inside of Anita, something that brings out another level of the character, specifically in her relation to Bernardo and María. She's a beautiful representation not only of Puerto Rican women today, but also of women in general and what we go through, how hard it is to take a stand for your own goals, your own beliefs and ambitions. And Steven is right: I am Anita. Of course, I've been getting from people, "Well, you know . . . Rita Moreno will always be my favorite Anita." And I agree. I just hope that there is a little bit of space for what I've done.

DAVID ALVAREZ: The rehearsals were a brotherhood and sisterhood of actors learning something to enhance themselves as artists. We all came from different backgrounds and different levels of experience. Tony Kushner was there during rehearsals. What is special about him is that he learns about you. He first sees you and he starts to think of how you connect with the character he wrote, and he'll adapt things depending on the person who is doing the role. I had a lot of input and listened to Tony and Steven, and we collaborated together to create one unified vision for this role. Everything has a reason behind it. The scar, for instance—Bernardo got it from a broken beer bottle during a fight. We had a discussion on whether we should have it or not, but we decided that it showed he was a fighter and, in fact, a boxer. Having been in the military myself, I know that when you're in that environment, you're going to get punched in the face, you're going to have scars everywhere, and if you're a fighter, it should show. The part that

we didn't have much rehearsal for was the acting aspect; that came on the day, on set. The really cool thing about working with Steven is that he's open to see what you can bring first and then he molds you to what his final vision is.

ANSEL ELGORT: Within that process was also the vocal rehearsals and getting the songs on a technical level, but also where they fit emotionally into the story. It's about the words, and it's about what you're trying to communicate; that's what Jeanine [Tesori, supervising vocal producer] is so great at doing. She's almost like an acting coach. She wanted to make sure that we got to the heart of what we were saying in the songs and made sure we got it in our voice.

Concept art of the Lincoln Center construction site by Alexios Chrysikos

JEANINE TESORI (supervising vocal producer): One of the things about working with Rachel and Ansel was not using words like "iconic," and trying not to remind them constantly of the legacy of this musical; I wanted them to really walk in with complete innocence. The songs, the feelings, had to feel new to them, just like they are for the characters.

ANSEL ELGORT: Stephen Sondheim came to rehearsals, to the prerecord of the songs, and talked to us all, gave great advice. He explained that when he writes lyrics, it's all about simplicity and then allowing the music to lift those simple words into, hopefully, an elevated place. He also said that Jerome Robbins was the only genius he ever met.

During that process one day, I kept saying, "Let me go back and rerecord 'María,' let me go back and rerecord 'Something's Coming.'" We did it many, many times. It was good, but it wasn't magic. At the end of the day, I found myself with Sondheim in the elevator, and he said nothing to me except "The most important thing a performer has is confidence." Perhaps that day I hadn't been confident enough in who I was as Tony and in singing the songs. I'm glad that he wasn't just nice to me and patted me on the back or said, "Good job," because ever since he said that, I've made sure that I have my confidence in what I'm doing and never let the pressure of Stephen Sondheim or Steven Spielberg being there influence my performance.

MIKE FAIST (Riff): I remember after the first day of rehearsal, when all the Jets were there, we all went to a bar up the street. We said to each other, "This is our story, and this is going to be an opportunity to tell it how we want to do it." We have to make sure that nothing is artificial. Nothing is put on about us or our relationship. We made a pact with one another to do these little hangout sessions, what we call "Jetivities," where everybody would choose an activity. Everyone agreed to do it. And right before we started shooting, the Shark boys and the Jet boys rented a house upstate in Rhinebeck; we spent the weekend together, played games, hung out, had a huge water balloon fight and just enjoyed each other and everyone's company.

GARETT HAWE (Skink): We had a lot of work sessions as the Jets, coming up with the relationships between each other, who knew each other before joining the Jets, and how each of us got into the Jets. Tony Kushner was incredibly helpful with differentiating our relationships. We rehearsed this project like a theater piece. There was a lot of trial and error in terms of what the choreography would be. And there were a lot of adjustments on the day of filming. You have to be able to roll with the punches.

JULIAN ELIA (Tiger): It's been interesting to have this two-month rehearsal period where we were incubating the whole thing, just learning how to live it, become it, and we were fully integrated, Jets and Sharks—I know that it wasn't the case for the cast of the original movie. Both groups were kept separate.

TALIA RYDER (Tessa): I remember being nervous on the first day of rehearsal. I recall first being welcomed by the Jets boys; they had already been working for a couple of weeks. They were laid-back and relaxed, which immediately put me at ease. Everyone was very helpful— Justin [Peck], Patti [Delgado], and Craig [Salstein] were amazing with us; I had never danced at that level, and Patti was particularly helpful in building my confidence. She always took the time to thoroughly explain her notes and to express her trust in us as dancers.

PATRICIA DELGADO: We worked with all sixty young dancers/actors for over two months to train them and create a company that would dance in unison. Thirty Sharks and thirty Jets. I learned very quickly that I would have to communicate with each group very differently. In order for both groups to understand the details and style and the nuance of Justin's choreography, I would have to get creative in my style of delivery. The Jets, most of whom came to the project with very versatile dance training and performance experience, related to counts and direct spatial notes while the Sharks responded better to corrections filled with imagery that they could relate to, like

Costume sketch of Maria by Miodrag Guberinic

sizzling hot oil in a sauté pan that starts to pop when you begin frying the *platanos*. If I gave them that sort of image to respond to, they knew exactly how to add a layer of attack and crisp spice to the movement that Justin was craving.

KYLE COFFMAN (Ice): Ansel was with us, taking ballet and dance class. And for us, that's the easy part. For him, it was more of a challenge, since he had to do an intense amount of training in just a few months, whereas we'd had years and years to train. On the other hand,

when we got on set, we were watching him as someone who'd been around the film industry and knows exactly what he's doing.

DAVID ALVAREZ: *War Against All Puerto Ricans* talks about all the things that people have gone through in Puerto Rico and how they've never really, truly been free. And I decided to write on my sneakers *Libertad* and drew the Puerto Rican flag on them with a light blue marker to match the original Puerto Rican flag, not the dark blue that it was changed to later. *Viva la revolución, viva Puerto Rico*

Concept art of the "Cool" set by Alexios Chrysikos

libre; that's what I think Bernardo feels every day; every time I look down at my shoes, I'm immediately in the moment.

PALOMA GARCIA-LEE (Graziella): Graziella is that real New York broad who chews gum and who is super tough and smokes, but we didn't want to make a caricature. We really wanted to make it truly her; she's a street girl. She's a bad girl, and we worked on how that informed my accent, my posture, how I worked with the Jet boys, her familiarity with the men, especially having dated Tony and now Riff. She likes to date the leaders of the gangs. She is not just a bimbo who sits back. She's in on what they're up to, she knows when they're fighting. She calls them out. She has this very strong and knowing presence, and the boys respect that about her; we built that camaraderie between her and the Jets. She has her right-hand girl, Velma, played by Maddie Ziegler, and it was really fun developing our friendship from the very beginning. Everyone adopted these characters and lived them. The boys spent a summer just completely immersed in each other's lives. And the girls did the same. So, when the camera started rolling, we just got to play.

THOM JONES (dialect coach): I had worked on *Ready Player One* with Steven, and they called me up and asked if I would be the dialect coach for *West Side Story*. I said I would love to and could certainly teach the New York accents, but I knew we were going to need to

have a Puerto Rican coach as well. Someone with the proper background and a connection to the culture. I suggested Victor Cruz, who had been a student of mine, is fluent in Spanish, and is also an actor. He turned out to be the perfect choice. Early on in the process, Victor and I put together very extensive files of sounds for Steven, specific samples from old films, even old interviews with public figures.

ANSEL ELGORT: My father's accent is basically the way I'm performing Tony. It's New York. My father was born in Washington Heights in 1940. By 1957, when the story takes place, Tony is maybe eighteen, nineteen; my dad was seventeen. I figured, *This is perfect*; I just took that voice, added a little more toughness to it and depth. But I've been hearing it my whole life, and I didn't even know it. I always just thought, *Oh, that's my dad's accent, and that is the New York accent that they want for this*.

VICTOR CRUZ (dialect coach): Some of the cast members are Puerto Rican, and some didn't speak Spanish. One of their biggest fears was that they would not be Puerto Rican enough. To help, I had them read short stories, newspaper articles in Spanish in front of a mirror. We worked on different pieces from the beginning so that they became comfortable with the language. It's like muscle training, and very quickly they connected back with their ancestry and DNA.

TALIA RYDER: During our breaks, I noticed that some of the cast would play Hacky Sack—I'd never played before, and, without any hesitation, they all welcomed me in and taught me—although it was a bit of a challenge in the dance heels.

When this process began, I had three hours of school each day at the dance studio, since I was still a junior in high school. I remember taking a chemistry final one day when we were rehearsing for "Dance at the Gym."

Watching Steven during rehearsal was fascinating—I was very curious and asked him about his process. He explained he was storyboarding the sequence and framing out shots. . . . He always took the time to answer questions, always made us feel valued.

On our last day of rehearsal, we all went to a restaurant near the studio—within two weeks, we felt like old friends. We couldn't wait to start filming.

ANSEL ELGORT: We did a publicity photo shoot before production started. It was nice to get a camera pointed at us and to start testing things out. It's really a luxury to do a shoot like that, because you get to dress up and be the character for a day and see how it feels. For instance, I realized my hair was too much to the side—I wanted to push it straight back and make it a little darker. We made some adjustments to the costumes, and we decided to have Tony in sneakers instead of dress shoes.

EZRA MENAS (Anybodys): During rehearsals, we would circle up and just kick the hack around whenever we had a spare moment. Just being able to chat and get to know one another really helped us. By the time we were at the photo shoot, the playfulness was already there. Mike [Faist] was always working with us on our New York accent, and had us stay in character, even at the photo shoot.

JANUSZ KAMINSKI (director of photography): Coming to rehearsals was essential for me, because I was able to develop a bond with the cast, and I also realized the physical aspect of the film, and how we could start thinking about capturing the dance numbers with the camera.

We are traveling with them. We are watching them as the dance is unveiling, and we're moving with them, and we're making creative choices to

David Alvarez's Libertad sneakers

see their expression. The physicality of the choreography was essential, to show the obvious vitality of these people, the vitality of their youth and, eventually, the rage. Without the rehearsals, we wouldn't have been able to fully understand how to approach those moments.

Essentially it is a very intimate story. This guy is falling in love with someone of a different culture, and it's the beginning of the tragedy. The actors are amazing. Rachel Zegler and Ariana DeBose are mind-blowing. And then, of course, Ansel (I call him "the kid," because he's such a youthful character) is amazing. To see all of them become those characters, even during rehearsals, was just beautiful. There was this chemistry between the actors. They loved each other's company, and they appreciated each other. It's very hard for people who are outside that particular profession to understand. It's almost a secret bond, and they feel the best among themselves, because they can be free. And also watching all the dancers, it was spectacular how noncompetitive they were, how sweet, tolerant, funny, and joyful they all were. They're all from Broadway; sometimes between takes, they would go into other musicals, and it was a really, really great experience to see the camaraderie.

Costume sketch of Maria by Miodrag Guberinic

THE ORCHESTRA

STEVEN SPIELBERG (director/producer): Prerecording the music was practically a first for me. I remember on *Close Encounters* we prerecorded the musical dialogue with the mothership a few times because that was part of a scene, but most of the time I'm just making the movie, and then I give it to John Williams, he goes off, writes the score, and then we spend about ten days in the recording studio when the film is all cut together. But this being a musical, it's a completely different approach.

Even when John Williams is doing scores for one of my films, I never stand on the conductor's podium. But before we started recording the music, in New York, with Gustavo Dudamel and the New York Philharmonic, I felt I had to thank everyone, and so I spoke from the podium. It was such a thrill, a great privilege and honor to be able to record Leonard Bernstein's monumental score with his orchestra. The recording sessions on West 34th Street were a blast. We had a lot of visitors, including John Williams, my wife [Kate Capshaw], several of my kids, many of our cast members including Rita, Rachel, Ansel, David, and Ariana. I wanted to be able to share our first evening of the recording session with President Barack Obama, who came with Michelle. Bruce Springsteen and his wife, Patti Scialfa, were also there. I got to spend a great deal of time with Steve Sondheim and the Bernstein siblings while we worked through the score. And maybe the biggest thrill of all was having Gustavo Dudamel conduct. It was John Williams's idea for me to ask Gustavo to conduct the entire score and it was one of John's many master strokes! Gustavo led the orchestra onto the movie screen with such insight, heart and dynamism, and his astounding musicianship.

JOHN WILLIAMS (music consultant): For Steven Spielberg's new film, the idea evolved to engage members of Leonard Bernstein's own former orchestra, the New

York Philharmonic, to record the score. [Due to Covid-19, additional orchestral recording of the score was done by the Los Angeles Philharmonic.] In very early discussions with Steven Spielberg, I suggested, and Steven agreed, that Gustavo Dudamel would be the best person to conduct Lenny's score for the new film. Gustavo is a brilliant artist, intimate with a broad range of symphonic repertoire while combining great experience with still-refreshing youth, and I felt immediately he would be the conductor most likely to bring a vigor and idiomatic freshness that would give the score new life. The resulting recording is a perfect balance of the breadth and sweep of the large film orchestration and the tighter sound of the original theater orchestration, with its characteristic swagger and swing.

DAVID NEWMAN (music arranger): How I got involved is through John Williams. I've known him for a long time—a few years ago, he started asking me to share the podium with him at the Hollywood Bowl; not every year, but it was quite an honor. I do the first half and he does the second half. I've written over a hundred scores for film, I've done quite a bit of conducting, I know *West Side Story* inside out, and John felt I had the background for this.

My title on the film is "Music arranged by." But I'm not really arranging as much as I'm there to supervise. I have a lot of experience with *West Side Story*. I've done the film with a live orchestra many times. In my twenties I did a semipro version of the show, and, believe it or not, I was involved in my high school production. I spent three months as a rehearsal pianist for *West Side Story*. I really got to know the piece at that time. And suddenly, this new movie came up. My job, as I see it, is to help keep things on track. I am working a lot with the Bernstein Estate to, basically, ensure the integrity and quality of the music. There are a few sequences in which I do need to arrange some of the music to underscore a scene, but there are very few examples of that. I've never done anything like this before. This is really a

Above
John Williams (music consultant) and Steven Spielberg

Opposite
Scoring session: Steven Spielberg, Gustavo Dudamel, and executive music producer/music supervisor Matthew Sullivan

huge musical collaboration with the Bernstein Office (especially Garth Edwin Sunderland, who is the vice president for creative projects with the Estate), Steven, John, Matt Sullivan, Joe E. Rand and Ramiro Belgardt, who are our music editors, Shawn Murphy, our scoring mixer and recordist, and of course, Gustavo Dudamel and the New York Philharmonic Orchestra.

Every piece of music and singing was prerecorded, but some singing was done live on set, and we ended up using pieces from both the prerecorded and the live performances, whichever one is best. As many people know, for instance, Richard Beymer's and Natalie Wood's singing voices were dubbed in the original *West Side Story*. In our new film, all the actors are singing and it's their own voice.

ALEXANDER BERNSTEIN (son of Leonard Bernstein): The New York Philharmonic of course has this great history with my father. He was the music director for all those years and made so many recordings with them, traveled the world with this orchestra, and there're still many musicians who played under his baton and knew him well. Gustavo Dudamel, though they never met, was able to channel my father's music. He got it like no one else. And being a Latin musician himself, he gets that sound so well. Dudamel was a perfect match.

GUSTAVO DUDAMEL (conductor): *West Side Story*, for me, as for all of us in the music world, is part of my DNA. Every single melody in it is so natural and easy for anyone to process . . . I discovered the piece when I was around fifteen years old. It was in a conducting class where we did some arrangements of "America" and "I Feel Pretty." The music conquered me immediately. It's so natural as a musician to feel connected to something that pure and unique, but you can also immediately identify that the story feels contemporary.

I have done a lot of the symphonic dances from *West Side Story*, like "The Mambo." And yes, I had heard that Steven Spielberg was considering doing a new film of it. Then one day, my assistant said, "You have a call that you have to take right now." It was Steven, his producer Kristie Macosko Krieger, and John Williams. They explained, "We want you to conduct the music of the new film." It was literally getting a call from heaven. Steven has a natural musical soul; he's a musician himself. And of course, we, including John Williams and David Newman, had many conversations throughout the process. Naturally, it felt right to work with the New York Philharmonic, Bernstein's own orchestra, and have the musicians be part of the new chapter of this masterpiece.

KRISTIE MACOSKO KRIEGER (producer): The recording sessions with the New York Philharmonic, and later with the LA Philharmonic, were some of the most exciting days for me as a producer. This film is a wonderful tribute to Leonard Bernstein's legacy, and on those days with the orchestra, it really felt like everything was starting to come together. It was such a joy to watch our cast lighting up to the music in that context.

ANSEL ELGORT (Tony): When we were singing the "Quintet," Dudamel said, "This is good, but think of it as a cake. When you buy a cake, you don't buy it already cut. You buy a full cake, and you only cut when you need a piece." And what he was saying is that I was taking these big breaths and unnecessary cuts where I should be making it a smooth "[slice of] cake." That analogy has stuck with me; I think about it all the time when I'm doing songs now.

GUSTAVO DUDAMEL: You need a technical way to explain things. But beyond that is imagination. The conductor has the responsibility to inspire; that's very important to me and why I use metaphors.

JAMIE BERNSTEIN (daughter of Leonard Bernstein): At the end of one of the takes of the song "America," Mr. Obama, who was sitting right next to me, leaned over and said, "Pretty good stuff, right?" I was speechless and just went, "Uh-huh." He reached over and squeezed my hand. I thought, *This is just the best moment of my whole life.*

RITA MORENO (Valentina): I turned around and there are Michelle and Barack Obama. And if that wasn't enough, I turned to my left, and there's Bruce Springsteen and Patti Scialfa, his wife. I was thrilled because I had someone musical in Bruce I could talk to about all the songs. It was wonderful. A night to remember.

RACHEL ZEGLER (María): I met Michelle first, and she gave me this big hug. She knew my name, asked about my birthday [which had just happened]. Then she went, "Barack, meet Rachel." He clearly loves this musical. He loves the music of *West Side Story*. He knows it so well. He was talking to Rita about it. And he was talking to Steven about what we were going to do with "America." He was also singing "María" to me in front of Ansel. It was surreal.

PATRICIA DELGADO (associate choreographer): The first time we heard the full orchestra sound was at the recordings, which took place just before we started filming. The music was filled with so much gusto and felt so alive that the dancers in attendance could not help but jump to their feet during "America" and "Dance at the Gym." For me, it was daunting to think we were going to leave the safe rehearsal space where we had spent so many weeks perfecting the choreography and we could always use more time to continue refining and making it better! I think it was the very necessary experience I needed to witness, to see these dancers so wild and free and excited by the fullness of the music, to know that they were ready for the filming to begin! So this was just a beautiful send-off.

Recording session with Gustavo Dudamel, conducting the New York Philharmonic Orchestra

FILMING BEGINS

KRISTIE MACOSKO KRIEGER (producer): Instead of adding an extra day onto our shooting schedule, we kicked off production with a pre-shoot on the evening of June 7, 2019. We shot scenes leading up to "The Rumble," including a section of the "Quintet." This was the first time the crew was together on set with the cast in costume; the atmosphere was electric and full of excitement (and occasionally, nerves). Our Sharks and Jets—many of whom were shooting their first feature film—just couldn't believe they were finally on set. But there's always some level of anxiety when we start a new film. There is so much involved logistically in getting it set up and running. . . . Yet Steven is a fearless leader and captain for the entire cast and crew. We all put our trust and faith in him and his vision, and again, on this occasion, he brought out the best in everyone.

EZRA MENAS (Anybodys): Before the official first day of filming, we had a pre-shoot day. I've never done a film before, so I was anxious. The scene took place after Tony has run away from the rumble. He had just killed Bernardo; Anybodys is searching for him, wants to take care of him, and try to prevent him from being arrested. It was a night scene. I went to set at midnight. Steven had chosen this rail yard that had all these abandoned train cars. I remember the atmosphere being so quiet. It was taxing emotionally, and yet so cool. I have a page of notes on my phone of all the things that Steven said to me that night. At the end of the night, Steven leaned over to me and said, "Congratulations, you just finished your first official shoot on a feature film," and shook my hand. Steven really takes the time to make those moments memorable for people. He has so much trust in the actor, and what the actor brings. In return, you have to really throw yourself into the work. You have to trust yourself.

HARRISON COLL (Numbers): The day of pre-filming for the Jets was the "Quintet" scene with the Jets walking across the tracks of a rail yard. It was June 7, 2019—my dad's birthday. There were so many emotions that day, but mostly I was thrilled to be paying tribute to my father's memory in a such a special way. My dad loved filmmaking and had an eye for design, and he would have been over the moon to know every detail about the set and the ins and outs of Steven's plan for shooting the scenes. I would've loved to share the experience with him and to have introduced him to one of his idols, the great Steven Spielberg. I did everything I could to channel his spirit during every moment of this incredible journey. On the day we wrapped I spoke to Steven about how much the experience meant to me and particularly how it reconnected me with the memory of my father. I told him how I wished my dad could have met him. I will never forget what Steven said: "Harrison, I have met him; I met him through you. His spirit lives on in you."

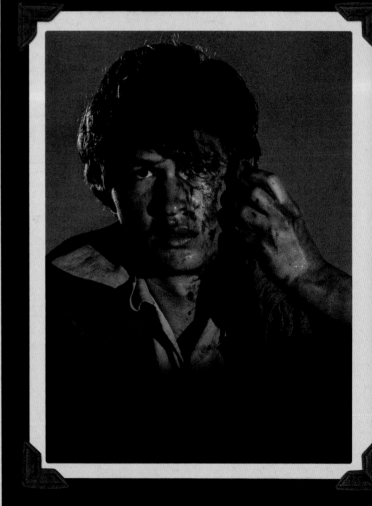

This page, top and bottom
Filming begins: Mike Faist (Riff) and Ansel Elgort (Tony)

Opposite, top and bottom
Sharks on the warpath

"PROLOGUE"

> EXT. LINCOLN CENTER, MANHATTAN — DAY
>
> No overture: Silence or street noise. The Screen is filled with a beautiful rendering of Lincoln Center. The camera pulls back to reveal that this rendering is part of a huge sign, captioned, above and below the painting: FUTURE HOME OF LINCOLN CENTER FOR THE PERFORMING ARTS.
>
> —from the script by Tony Kushner

STEVEN SPIELBERG (director/producer): The one thing that unites the two gangs, the Jets and the Sharks, is that they share a neighborhood that's being torn down. The movie starts with an image of Lincoln Center, and I want the audience to think, Oh my God, the movie takes place in 2020! But, in fact, we reveal that it's just a beautiful artist's rendering of what Lincoln Center is going to look like; the camera cranes up and we see that everything has been demolished. This is a slum story about slum clearance. These kids are fighting for territory that's disappearing before their eyes.

VIRGINIA SÁNCHEZ KORROL (historical consultant): Under Robert Moses, who chaired the Mayor's Committee on Slum Clearance right after World War II, New York City was prime for urban renewal. New York was becoming a financial center. The city had turned to a consumer economy and actively recruited workers. At the same time, a great migration of Puerto Ricans were coming to the city from the archipelago, seeking jobs. Puerto Rico was undergoing massive industrialization changes. Jobs declined drastically, and the agricultural sector became stagnant. The migrants were American citizens who already had a long

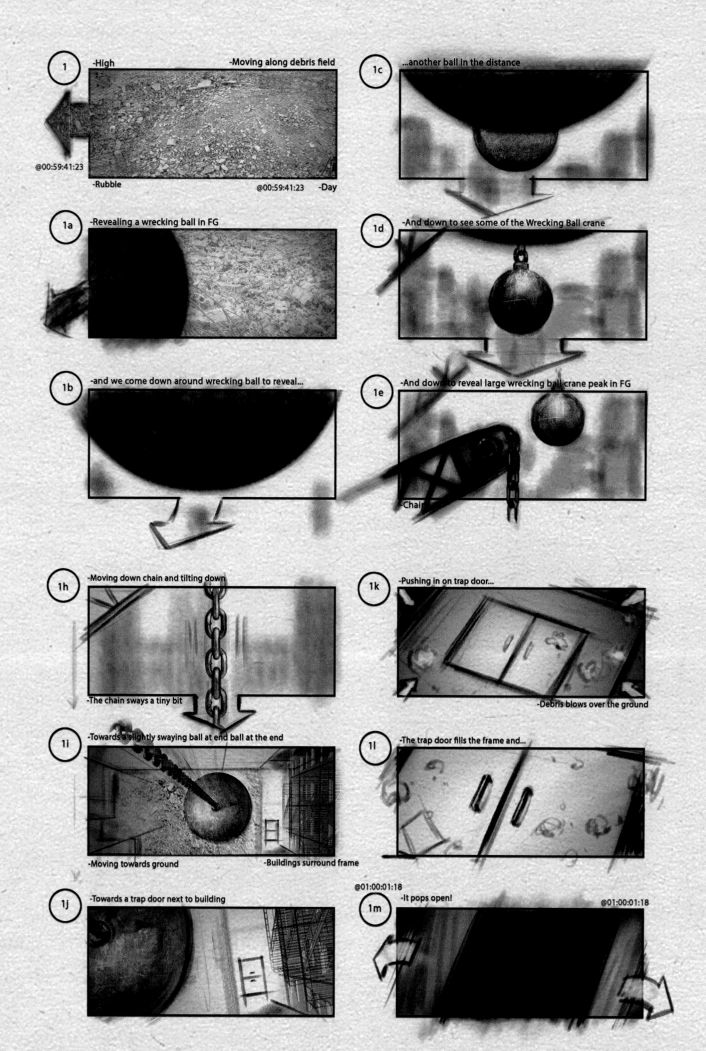

Storyboards by Raymond Prado

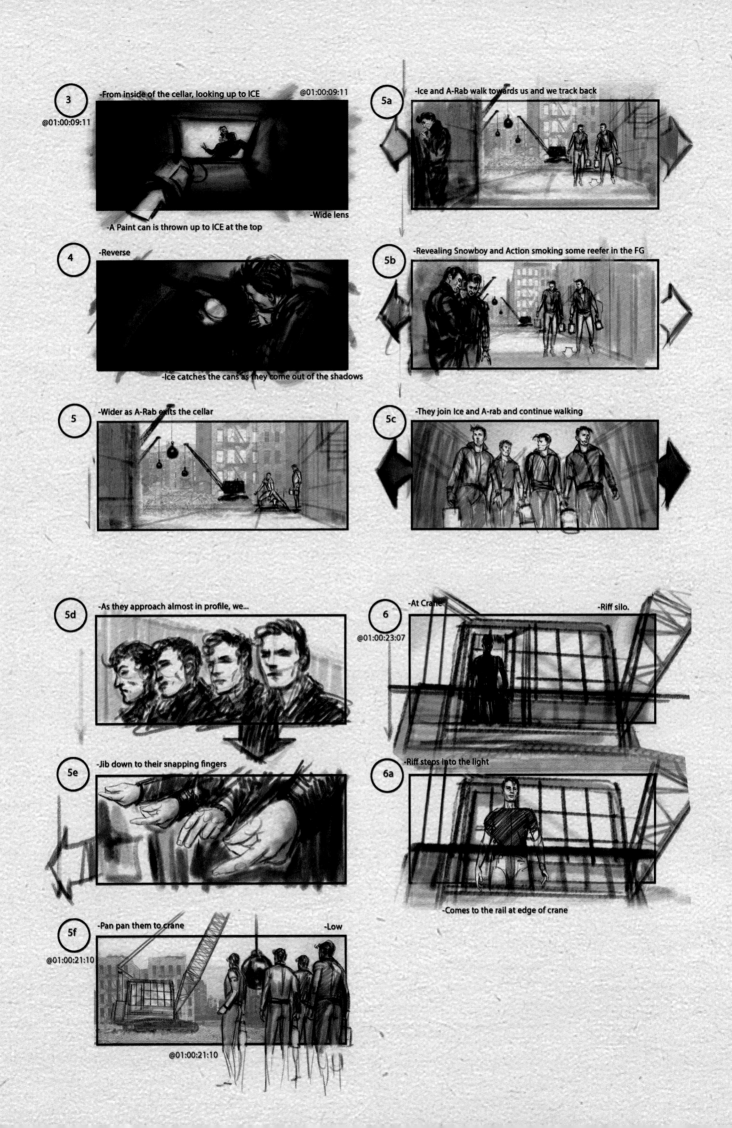

3 @01:00:09:11

-From inside of the cellar, looking up to ICE @01:00:09:11

-Wide lens

-A Paint can is thrown up to ICE at the top

4 -Reverse

-Ice catches the cans as they come out of the shadows

5 -Wider as A-Rab exits the cellar

5a -Ice and A-Rab walk towards us and we track back

5b -Revealing Snowboy and Action smoking some reefer in the FG

5c -They join Ice and A-rab and continue walking

5d -As they approach almost in profile, we...

5e -Jib down to their snapping fingers

5f -Pan pan them to crane -Low
@01:00:21:10
@01:00:21:10

6 @01:00:23:07 -At Crane -Riff silo.

6a -Riff steps into the light

-Comes to the rail at edge of crane

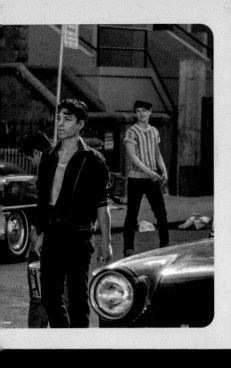

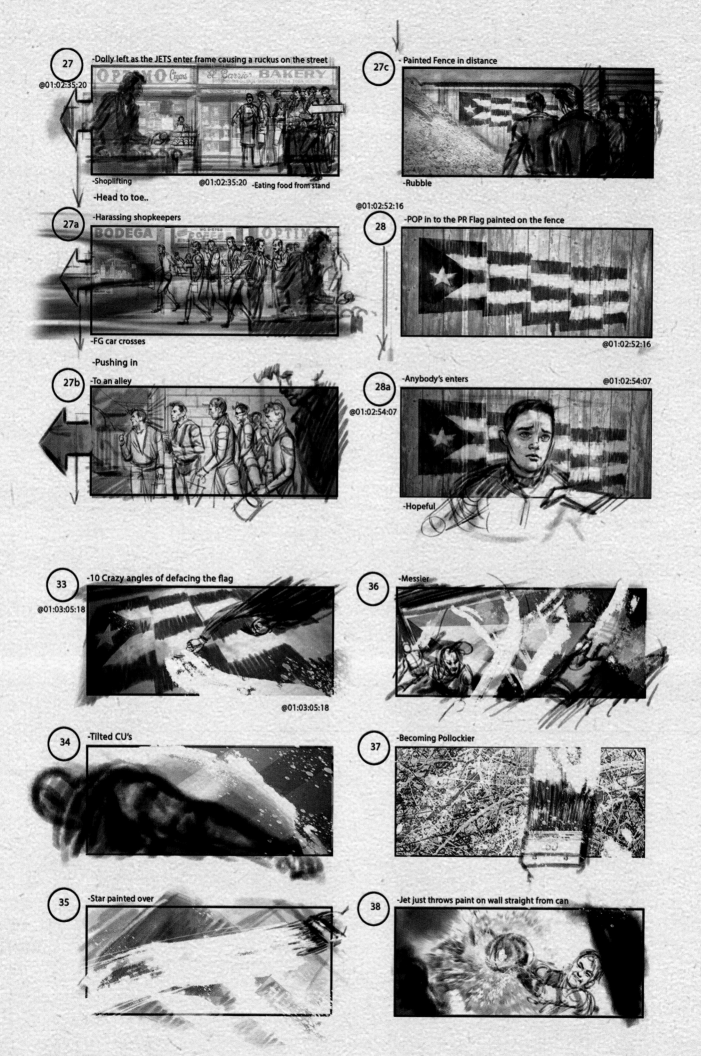

27 @01:02:35:20 -Dolly left as the JETS enter frame causing a ruckus on the street

-Shoplifting

-Head to toe..

-Eating food from stand @01:02:35:20

27a -Harassing shopkeepers

-FG car crosses

-Pushing in

27b -To an alley

27c - Painted Fence in distance

-Rubble

@01:02:52:16

28 -POP in to the PR Flag painted on the fence

@01:02:52:16

28a -Anybody's enters @01:02:54:07

@01:02:54:07

-Hopeful

33 @01:03:05:18 -10 Crazy angles of defacing the flag

@01:03:05:18

34 -Tilted CU's

35 -Star painted over

36 -Messier

37 -Becoming Pollockier

38 -Jet just throws paint on wall straight from can

Storyboards by Raymond Prado

history in the United States. Many were veterans of the war, and some even had long-standing familial ties dating to the twenties and thirties.

Coming home from elementary school one afternoon, I still remember the horrific encounter with enormous rats I found scavenging on top of the stove. Because tenements around us were being demolished, vermin and roaches fled the bulldozed buildings for housing that was still intact.

I spoke to the cast about how it feels to be a child undergoing urban renewal, which meant your family had to move. And that your neighborhood was being destroyed. And by destroying a neighborhood, you take away leadership. You take away the stores, the pharmacist, the schools, doctors, friends and family.

JANUSZ KAMINSKI (director of photography): The fire-escape structures are an essential part of the story. This is where Tony and María fall in love, this is where the first kiss happens, and as we know, it all ends tragically. Steven pretty much had a solid cut of the film shortly after we completed photography. And he called explaining he wanted to do some additional filming to bring broken fire escapes right at the beginning of the title sequence; we're looking at the city as it's changing, with the broken fire escapes; we're craning past them and going into the buildings that are being destroyed by the renovation project. Clearly, the broken fire escapes are the metaphor that hint at broken lives, broken relationships. That's the art of directing.

JUSTIN PECK (choreographer): "Prologue" is an incredibly important moment in our film. It's where we first introduce the language of dance that runs through the film, as a means of expression, of communication, of emotion, of camaraderie, of power, of tension, of conflict. The way we approached the introduction of this language is not unlike how Jerome Robbins originally did it—by very slowly easing into dance movement. This "slow boil" allows the audience's eyes and minds to adjust to the tool of expression and guides them to embrace the movement expression that courses through the film.

Previous
Ezra Menas (Anybodys) pursued by the Sharks

Above
Sharks and Jets battle for territory.

Opposite
David Alvarez (Bernardo)

I remember shooting one section that involved three of the Jets: Harrison Coll as Numbers, Jess LeProtto as A-Rab, and Ben Cook as Mouthpiece. They had to glide, like synchronized ice-skaters, diagonally down a sloped street, between cars, moving onto the pavement and then back up onto the sidewalk, all while supporting one another and staying in character and maintaining their cool. It was incredibly challenging, and we shot it on one of the hottest days out in Paterson, New Jersey (nearly 100 degrees). The guys were so determined to nail it, and Steven and I really embraced their tenacity. We must have shot this one-er about thirteen or fourteen times before getting an acceptable take that we were all happy with. But it was entirely worth it— it is one of the most unexpectedly gorgeous moments in the film.

CRAIG SALSTEIN (associate choreographer): The "Prologue," to me, was about Justin finding the vocabulary, the sound of the Jets, the words through movement.

MATTHEW SULLIVAN (executive music producer/music supervisor): The "Prologue" really is a musical number of its own, because there is no lyric, and no dialogue. So the music has to tell the story, along with the visuals. We spent a huge part of preproduction working with Steven on how we were going to tell the story of the Jets and the Sharks with the existing music, extend it a bit to match Steven's visuals and get it approved by the Bernstein Estate. You have the Jets getting the paint cans, desecrating the Puerto Rican flag, and the Sharks chasing them. We had to get all that story in, and the music had to match exactly what the action was. We may have done up to forty different versions of the music, doing some small tweaks here and there, a lot of trial and error to just get it all correct.

KEVIN CSOLAK (Diesel): The "Prologue" starts with Ice, Action, Diesel, and A-Rab doing

The Jets! From left: Kevin Csolak (Diesel), Patrick Russell (Little Moly), Kyle Allen (Balkan), Kyle Coffman (Ice), Ben Cook (Mouthpiece), Mike Faist (Riff), John Michael Fiumara (Big Deal), Jess LeProtto (A-Rab)

a task for Riff as he assembles the Jets. Justin gave us an incredible arc of movement for it. It starts very minuscule. It commences with a simple gesture and breaks into dance, and both are seamlessly unified.

KYLE COFFMAN (Ice): I have been practicing snapping my fingers since I was a kid. When we actually went to record it in the booth, and it was time to put your fingers up to the microphone, we became nervous and our fingers got all sweaty. We were looking at each other, trying to get it on the beat, and eventually got it right.

ANDREI CHAGAS (Jochi): One day, after shooting a very dark moment in "Prologue," I was watching the video playback next to Steven, and he said how important the two months of rehearsals had been, because of the bond we created. . . . He explained how it definitely showed on camera.

MIKE FAIST (Riff): The "Prologue" is showing what has been going on, and where these guys are now, how tense it is getting. It is the beginning of the buildup between the Jets and the Sharks, and it shows the dynamic between the two gangs. . . . You see the Jets, who are going around and terrorizing the neighborhood. It almost seems like a regular thing they do: "What kind of mischief can we get ourselves involved in with the Sharks today?"

And it just so happens that they're going to deface this mural, with the Puerto Rican flag.

BEN COOK (Mouthpiece): In the context of the "Prologue," the Jets have a clear intention: They're moving through the streets and approach a Puerto Rican flag on a mural in the Sharks' territory. They have paint cans, brushes, and they deface it. The second we took a step back and looked at what we actually were doing was when it all sunk in. It's the start of a much deeper conflict.

VIRGINIA SÁNCHEZ KORROL: The rivalry between the two gangs is very realistic. In fact, I know it was something that was already happening when my father came to New York at sixteen during the 1920s. Coming home from work, he had to cross through a gang-controlled Italian neighborhood. Growing up, I would bombard him with questions about how he managed to escape, and he would explain, "Well, I had to run like hell." And this continues to happen with present-day gangs. The gang or turf wars in *West Side Story* are very real, because marginalized communities fight to protect what they call home.

GARY RYDSTROM (re-recording mixer/ sound designer): To have an opening like this, that slowly reveals the place the movie is set, is a gift to the sound editors on the movie.

Opposite
Concept art by Hugh Sicotte

It involves our sense of what's around us—in this case construction, or deconstruction, in 1957 New York. The sound gets to slowly reveal where we are and what's going on. This is something that Steven Spielberg films often do, this slow pulling of the audience into the world of the movie. In this case, the "Prologue" reveals the theme of the movie: the tearing down of the old to make way for the new. The characters of our movie are going to be in the middle of this transition, and that means that throughout the movie, we can hear that change happening off-screen and remind the audience of it.

In the "Prologue," and throughout this movie, the timing of the action to the music (integrating sounds from the real world with the rhythms of the number, the snaps was essential. We rerecorded finger snaps on the scoring stage up at Skywalker Ranch. . . .

There are no more important-sounding snaps in the history of movies than the ones for *West Side Story*.

There's an underlying sense of potential violence that's key to the whole story. For simple things early on, like the paint slapping on the wall—the paint that the Jets are painting over the Puerto Rican flag mural—we used a sound-editing trick and snuck in the sound of face slaps as the paint brushes and cloth are whipping and hitting the wall. That adds a sense of aggression and violence to something that you wouldn't normally get that feeling from in real life.

"LA BORINQUEÑA"

—an excerpt of the revolutionary version of the song by Lola Rodríguez de Tió

¡DESPIERTA, BORINQUEÑO
QUE HAN DADO LA SEÑAL!
¡DESPIERTA DE ESE SUEÑO
QUE ES HORA DE LUCHAR!
A ESE LLAMAR PATRIÓTICO
¿NO ARDE TU CORAZÓN?
¡VEN! NOS SERÁ SIMPÁTICO
EL RUIDO DEL CAÑÓN.
MIRA, YA EL CUBANO
LIBRE SERÁ;
LE DARÁ EL MACHETE
SU LIBERTAD . . .
LE DARÁ EL MACHETE
SU LIBERTAD.
YA EL TAMBOR GUERRERO
DICE EN SU SON,
QUE ES LA MANIGUA EL SITIO,
EL SITIO DE LA REUNIÓN,
DE LA REUNIÓN . . .
DE LA REUNIÓN.
EL GRITO DE LARES
SE HA DE REPETIR,
Y ENTONCES SABREMOS
VENCER O MORIR.
BELLÍSIMA BORINQUEN,
A CUBA HAY QUE SEGUIR;
TU TIENES BRAVOS HIJOS
QUE QUIEREN COMBATIR.

ARISE, PUERTO RICAN!
THE CALL TO ARMS HAS
SOUNDED!
AWAKE FROM THIS DREAM,
IT IS TIME TO FIGHT!
DOESN'T THIS PATRIOTIC
CALL SET YOUR HEART
ALIGHT?
COME, WE ARE IN TUNE WITH
THE ROAR OF THE CANNON.
COME, THE CUBAN WILL
SOON BE FREE;
THE MACHETE WILL GIVE HIM
HIS LIBERTY,
THE MACHETE WILL GIVE HIM
HIS LIBERTY.
NOW THE WAR DRUM
SAYS WITH ITS SOUND,
THAT THE JUNGLE IS THE
PLACE,
OF THE MEETING . . .
OF THE MEETING . . .
OF THE MEETING.
THE CRY OF LARES
MUST BE REPEATED,
AND THEN WE WILL KNOW:
VICTORY OR DEATH.
BEAUTIFUL PUERTO RICO
MUST FOLLOW CUBA;
YOU HAVE BRAVE SONS
WHO WISH TO FIGHT.

VIRGINIA SÁNCHEZ KORROL (historical consultant): "La Borinqueña" was written in the nineteenth century by Lola Rodríguez de Tió. It was the revolutionary song for one of the first uprisings in Puerto Rico in 1868. She was a poet, very well-known throughout the entire Spanish-speaking world. She had been asked to write something that would get people roused up, on their feet, and ready to fight a revolution. She adopted the popular dance music by Félix Astol Artés and wrote the revolutionary words. The uprising was aborted. Insurgents went into hiding or had to leave the island. It wasn't until the twentieth century that people began to realize this was a pivotal historical moment. The lyrics were altered in 1952, but the song continues to be identified by the island as its national anthem. It adds a great deal to the movie.

When I read in the script that Bernardo was singing "La Borinqueña," I thought, *Oh God, I love this!* But I questioned why he was singing it. How did he even know the revolutionary words to "La Borinqueña"? Most of the kids I grew up with would never have known that. Understanding my concern, Tony Kushner developed a backstory for Bernardo that I could relate to, and completely justified Bernardo's knowledge of the song. I believed in the authenticity of that character.

DAVID ALVAREZ (Bernardo): We got to shoot the scene the same week that actual protests were going on in Puerto Rico. It brought something quite real to that particular moment.

JACOB GUZMAN (Junior): That was one of the most powerful, moving moments.... Made us so proud to be Puerto Rican and to be representing Puerto Ricans in this movie.

DAVID AVILÉS MORALES (Aníbal): It felt really good singing our revolutionary anthem, and what it says really goes well with what's happening today in our country. Singing felt like such a relief. It's saying, "Wake up, see what is really happening with our country, fight for it and for that freedom." Thank you, Tony Kushner. Thank you, Steven Spielberg, for putting that anthem into the movie.

Left
Costume sketch of Bernardo by Shane Ballard

Opposite, top
Concept art by Alexios Chrysikos

Opposite, bottom
Bernardo (David Alvarez) faces off with the police: Officer Krupke (Brian d'Arcy James, center) and Lieutenant Schrank (Corey Stoll)

"JET SONG"

Riff goes up to each of the Jets, telling them
truths they already know, asking them to come back to
themselves.
—from the script by Tony Kushner

ADAM STOCKHAUSEN (production designer): Steven wanted the site of this demolition of the neighborhood to be an active part of the telling of the story. We quickly got this idea that the Jets' part of the neighborhood would be the one that had just been knocked down. We knew that we wanted the demolition site of the actual construction pit to be a big set in the movie. We talked about it being in a back lot; we talked about it being a stage set. But from the very beginning of our location scouting, we were looking for a site within a city, and we ended up finding a great space, two parking lots with a road in between, in Paterson, New Jersey. We also did this giant pile of rubble in the demolition lot where Steven wanted to end "Jet Song" with all them racing together up to the top of it. We had to have it look dangerous and covered with spiky bits of rusty metal and brick, but still have pads to keep it safe for the dancers to climb.

TONY KUSHNER (screenwriter/executive producer): Stephen Sondheim is a genius—a word I use very rarely. Some of the lyrics for *West Side Story* have the brilliant rhyming and wordplay we associate with him, but some of them are simple. For instance, I knew "Jet Song" as a great introductory number, sharp and fun and funny, but after listening to it over and over I came to understand what I think the song is really about: It's an incisive analysis of the successive stages of teenage male group psychology. The first verse is about fear, insecurity, the negatives that bring the gang together and keep it together—the world is a

Mike Faist (Riff, foreground) leads the Jets: Ben Cook (Mouthpiece, center) and Kevin Csolak (Diesel, left).

dangerous place, and you need to belong, to be a Jet to survive. Once the gang has gathered, the boys feel secure, and the mood becomes celebratory and joyful—"You're the top cat in town." But beneath the joy, fueling it, is the lonely terror and vulnerability that engendered it, and this rises up in the third verse, making the celebration turn aggressive, violent, as these slum rats return to the world the violence it's visited on them.

Every song in *West Side Story* yields that kind of dramatic richness. None is static, each is a beautifully structured progression, each develops the characters, their relationships to each other and to language and class and history, each advances narrative and meaning.

MIKE FAIST (Riff): "Jet Song" is about the Jets questioning everything and thinking about disbanding and walking away. The entire "Jet Song" is to try to get these guys back to what's important, which is each other, family— basically, the only thing that they really know, the only thing that's really been keeping each other safe. There's this amazing book that we were all reading called *The Shook-Up Generation* by Harrison E. Salisbury (1967) where this journalist in the mid- to late fifties went around to all the New York City youth gangs and interviewed them, hung out with them, and got to know them as individuals. You see where these boys and girls are coming

from. They have nothing. They talk about how the society at the time is not helping them to find stable footing. They have nothing to look forward to, and so, as a result, they cling to each other and pick a common enemy and just say, "This section is ours." They'll fight for a mound of dirt, because it's something tangible that they can claim and have control over, even though they have no control over their own life. At the end of the song, when you see that shot of the Jets on top of rubble, celebrating and putting figuratively the flag into the dirt, staking their territory, you actually understand as well the bond between them.

DANIEL PATRICK RUSSELL (Little Moly): We all climbed down from the rubble after we did the shot and ran to the tent, where Steven played back the take for us, and he was so ecstatic. Steven said to us that we had staked our flag, and that this was officially our version of *West Side Story*.

Opposite
From left: Ice (Kyle Coffman), Riff (Mike Faist), Diesel (Kevin Csolak)

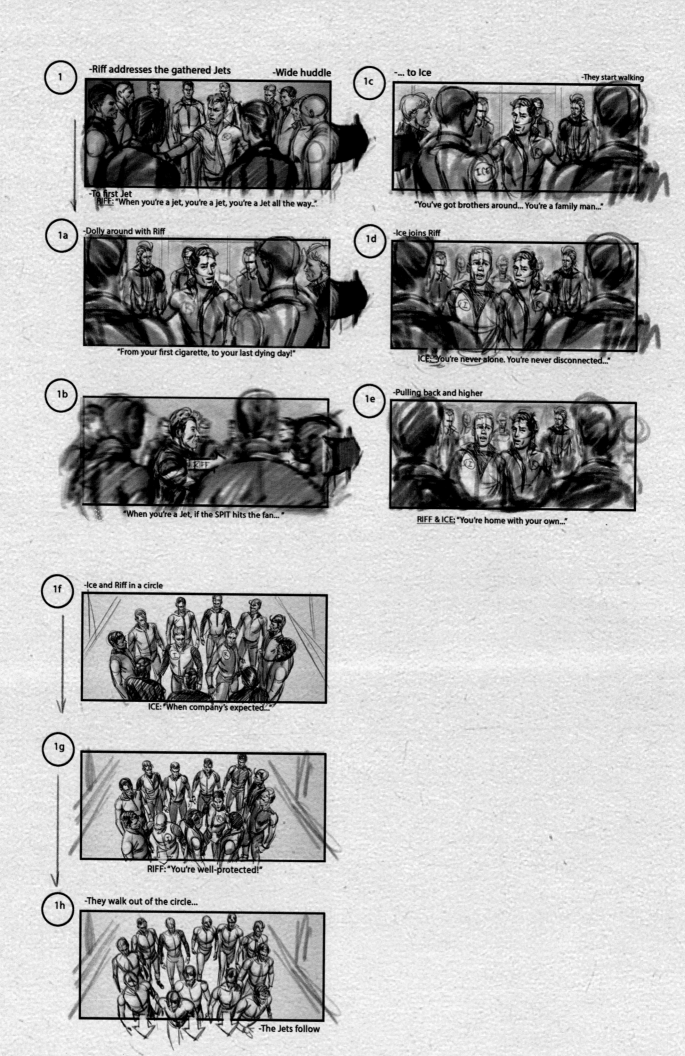

1 — -Riff addresses the gathered Jets · -Wide huddle
-To first Jet
RIFF: "When you're a jet, you're a jet, you're a Jet all the way..."

1c — -... to Ice · -They start walking
"You've got brothers around... You're a family man..."

1a — -Dolly around with Riff
"From your first cigarette, to your last dying day!"

1d — -Ice joins Riff
ICE: "You're never alone. You're never disconnected..."

1b
"When you're a Jet, if the SPIT hits the fan..."

1e — -Pulling back and higher
RIFF & ICE: "You're home with your own..."

1f — -Ice and Riff in a circle
ICE: "When company's expected..."

1g
RIFF: "You're well-protected!"

1h — -They walk out of the circle...
-The Jets follow

"SOMETHING'S COMING"

> . . . Tony is torn: [Valentina's] right, he feels a
> new kind of hopefulness; but he's also afraid to give
> in to it because in his whole difficult life, nothing
> great has ever come his way before. He's caught between
> possibility and doubt.
> —from the script by Tony Kushner

STEVEN SPIELBERG (director/producer): Doc's is the drugstore where
Tony sings "Something's Coming" to Valentina. In the other productions, Tony sings
all of his songs solo. In our film, he expresses himself to strangers and to people he
loves.

Valentina is trying to get Tony to pick himself up and start over again. She
gives him the confidence that launches him into the song "Something's Coming." We
noticed that even though the song—which I believe was the last song Bernstein and
Sondheim wrote, it was added in previews—is optimistic and forward looking, it's
full of questions like "Could it be?" and uncertainties like "Who knows?" Our version
of Tony is a gang leader who's done time for nearly committing a murder. He's had
a very hard life already, even though he's young. Inside him, hope and despair are
always in conflict.

TONY KUSHNER (screenwriter/ executive producer): Arthur Laurents wrote Tony as a good kid from a nice, intact family who's trying to keep his life on the straight and narrow; he's somehow innately different from the members of his former gang. I wanted to explore what constituted that difference, what had happened to Tony that made his path diverge from Riff and the Jets. So, I took away his intact family and gave him the same troubled, violent, orphaned childhood as the other Jets; but something has happened to him that's changed him: Seventeen months before the story begins, Tony almost killed a kid from another gang, and he's spent a year in state prison. During this enforced separation from his pals, he's had to face himself and his near brush with committing murder. It's wrought a profound change in him.

ANSEL ELGORT (Tony): Tony is Polish, but he got into a brawl with the Egyptian Kings, which is another gang from uptown. He got arrested because he hurt this kid really bad and went to jail. When the story begins, he's just out of prison and the Jets want Tony to come back. But Tony knows he can't.

The song "Something's Coming" starts as a pep talk to himself. Something will come and he can stay hopeful. . . . It's just around the corner. By the end of the song, Tony is convinced that it might just be tonight. And he heads off to the dance at the gym, which is where he meets María.

PAUL TAZEWELL (costume designer): Valentina is living as a widow outside of the norms of this changing city; she married someone who wasn't Latino, and that was a powerful act for that time. For Rita, it was imperative that Valentina not come off as a feeble old woman. We decided that Valentina is full of life and that her clothing should reflect that. Although she's been through a lot, she continues to be robust and very engaged in running the drugstore that was co-owned with her dead husband; I originally designed mostly dresses for her, and one of the suggestions that Rita made was that she would wear trousers in her first scene with Tony, to make her appear more active. Later, she is in a shirtwaist dress and smock to round out her wardrobe.

ANSEL ELGORT: To me, Rita symbolizes Hollywood. What's so impressive is that she's eighty-seven and she still moves like she just came out of dance class. Her voice sounds amazing. She sounds just as good now as she ever did. She is hilarious, has no shame, and is totally herself. She has great energy, and it rubbed off on all of us. It was a contagious good feeling, and Rita brings it with her wherever she goes.

Top
Steven Spielberg directs Mike Faist (Riff).

Bottom
Director of photography Janusz Kaminski frames a shot.

Following spread
Mike Faist (Riff) and Ansel Elgort (Tony) take direction from Steven Spielberg in the storeroom at Doc's.

AT HOME WITH MARÍA, ANITA, AND BERNARDO

STEVEN SPIELBERG (director/producer): Paul Tazewell and his costumes . . . Adam Stockhausen and his sets . . . We were surrounded by and standing inside their genius. It was all around us, and the realness, the historical authenticity of the sets down to the details of Anita, Bernardo, and María's apartment . . . It felt like musical and documentary as one.

DAVID ALVAREZ (Bernardo): The first time I understood what *West Side Story* meant was in 2009, when I was thirteen years old, while doing *Billy Elliot*. At the time, the *West Side Story* revival was playing on Broadway. I got to see it then, and when I won the Tony Award for *Billy Elliot*, I met the cast from *West Side*—I had immediately connected to the story because of its Shakespearian background but also because it's a story of love, fear, and how these two feelings are really in charge of everyone's lives. You have to choose what it is that you want to live by. On top of that, the music, the dancing, basically all these different art forms culminate into something so beautiful.

Bernardo is the leader of the Sharks gang, and he's from Puerto Rico; he's a boxer, and he came to America to make some money so he could go back to Puerto Rico and live a beautiful life with his family—that's his ultimate goal. The beautiful Anita is his girlfriend, and to Bernardo, she's a perfect representation of what a woman should be, and that's why he's so madly in love with her.

From left: Ariana DeBose (Anita), Rachel Zegler (María), and Steven Spielberg

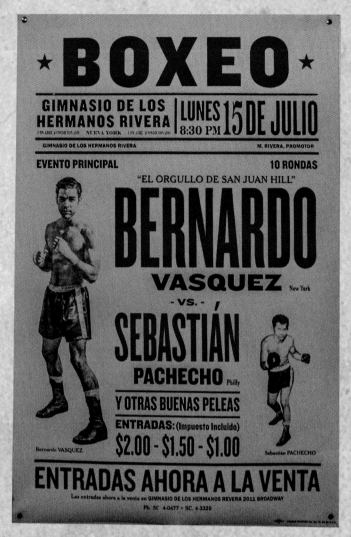

ARIANA DᴇBOSE (Anita): Our Anita is the life of the party, but she's also one of the smartest people in the room; you just don't happen to realize it until much later. She's the Earth. She is what grounds this piece in a big way. She brings the humanity to it. She's the consummate observer. She's a peacekeeper, but she is what brings the Sharks and the Puerto Rican storyline back to a home base, to family and love. She makes the story not only about survival but also about thriving in a new place. She makes it okay for these people to want more.

RACHEL ZEGLER (María): María Vasquez has been in New York for five months. She's a bit of a shut-in. She works at Gimbels. That's all she really does. She stays home all day. She works at night. She's really excited to go to the dance at the gym; she wants to meet people; she wants to fall in love. It's such a beautiful way to meet María as this teenage girl who just wants to have fun.

ARIANA DᴇBOSE: This is no longer just a male-centered story. With Tony Kushner's adaptation, the women have an essential role to play. They take center stage, and we are unapologetic about it. The views of the women in this story are important.

RACHEL ZEGLER: There is a scene where María wakes up after the balcony scene. She slept in her clothes, Anita calls for breakfast, and María rushes to make it look like she was in her pajamas. She messes her makeup and her hair. It's not a dance, but it's choreography. Justin Peck helped me do everything for that moment. It was filmed in one Steadicam shot, too, and he made me, who's a non-dancer, look like I knew what I was doing. It is so beautiful when you watch bodies telling a story without having to say anything. I really feel like that is what Justin Peck's choreography is. And that's in everything that he does.

This page
Boxing promo for a Bernardo bout

Opposite, top
David Alvarez (Bernardo) discusses his accent with dialect coach Victor Cruz.

Opposite, bottom
A light moment between Ariana DeBose (Anita) and Steven Spielberg

Following spread, top left **Ariana DeBose (Anita)**

Following spread, bottom left **Rachel Zegler (María)**

be on set in a new role. It was mind-blowing, watching the two of them together, talking, discussing, laughing. Rita embraced Ariana's performance, and Ariana made it clear how inspired she was by Rita. And Ariana is a great actress, a great singer and dancer—it's a cliché but she really lights up the whole screen, and when the story gets tragic, she breaks our hearts. There are so many couples in *West Side Story* that have to have chemistry: María and Tony of course, and Anita and Bernardo, but also Tony and Riff, and María and Anita. Rachel and Ariana as María and Anita were soulmates.

GARY RYDSTROM (re-recording mixer/sound designer): When we're at home with María and Anita and Bernardo, I wanted to give a sense with the sound of the thin walls of the apartment building they live in. We hear activity going on left and right and even above, people walking around, doors opening and closing, voices, babies crying. It was a big part of setting up the feeling of this kind of apartment.

One of my favorite sounds for an old apartment is refrigerators; they sounded louder and more interesting in those days. Later on, there's a scene where Anita is working her fabric and she puts newspapers on the floor, so that was a great touch for us to add a feeling of what it sounds like to walk around an apartment full of newspapers on the floor.

STEVEN SPIELBERG: Rachel and Ariana are both young women with old souls and tons of chutzpah mixed with pride and joy. Rachel walked on to this huge set, never having made a movie before, surrounded by a bunch of fairly formidable people and superbly talented actors with much more experience than her. She watched, she listened, she learned at a jaw-dropping rate, but she also brought with her that mysterious quality of having been born to do what she's doing. Her María is a revelation. Ariana had the difficult task of finding her own version of Anita, who had been incarnated so magnificently in the first film by Rita Moreno, who was going to

Previous spread, right
Bernardo (David Alvarez) chats with his sister, María (Rachel Zegler)

Above
Ariana DeBose (Anita) and David Alvarez (Bernardo)

Opposite
Rachel Zegler (María) between shots with Steven Spielberg

"DANCE AT THE GYM"

[The Shark girls and the Sharks] burst through the doors and enter the gym. In front of bleachers, near the punchbowls and snacks, a few male and female SOCIAL WORKERS in their 20s and 30s keep watch, along with four PATROLMEN positioned around the hall. Krupke, in charge, stands by the door, drinking coffee.

On a stage opposite the doors, African American, Puerto Rican and white MUSICIANS, The San Juan Hill Serenaders painted on a drum. The BAND LEADER's a cool Puerto Rican guy.

The JET GIRLS and the Jets are already there, jitterbugging athletically, fingers snapping. Riff and Graziella hold the center of the floor.

The Puerto Ricans stand near the door, unsure what to do with themselves, not liking the music or the dancing or the dancers. Bernardo leads Anita near the dance floor.

As the Jets continue to occupy the floor, the other Sharks start openly imitating what the gringo kids are doing.

—from the script by Tony Kushner

STEVEN SPIELBERG (director/producer): We wanted to differentiate between the Jets' and the Sharks' costumes in several ways. Our Jets are really street rats—drop-outs, unemployed, scavengers—as Lieutenant Schrank identifies them, they're the grandchildren of European immigrants who mostly moved up

and moved out—except for the parents of the Jets. The Sharks in our version are young Puerto Rican guys, many of them recent arrivals to New York, who've bonded together to protect their neighborhood from the nativist vandalism of groups like the Jets. They have jobs—probably each one holds a number of jobs—and they're trying to make it in the city. For the most part, the Jets dress more drably than the Sharks. We didn't want the kids on either side dressed uniformly—Paul Tazewell is extraordinary with details that give every single costume its individual character and history. The only time we decided to get a bit schematic is at the dance in the gym. Since the number is about cultural differences and about synthesizing, I wanted to be sure you can easily keep track of the Jets,

who are in blues and greens, and the Sharks, in reds and oranges. When the gangs segregate, there's a bold, startling rift on the dance floor. When those lines start to blur, the whole gym becomes a kind of rainbow.

KRISTIE MACOSKO KRIEGER (producer): If there's one number from this film people remember, I think it will be "Dance at the Gym." It was one of the most ambitious scenes in the film and involved a lot of moving parts and pieces, not to mention we filmed it in a Catholic school gymnasium with no air-conditioning! It features almost our entire cast—more than sixty dancers and 150 background actors—and the choreography was intricate and involved. That scene is so incredible, because the energy

Above
Choreographer Justin Peck, associate choreographer Craig Salstein, Steven Spielberg, and Clay Lerner (Steven Spielberg's production assistant)

Opposite
The Jets and Sharks face off at "Dance at the Gym."

just builds and builds as the two gangs compete with each other on the dance floor, but it eventually leads to Tony and María's fateful meeting. It's one of the most important scenes in the entire film, and the way the set, the costumes, the dancing, and the music came together was nothing short of magical. Everyone's creative contribution, Janusz's photography, Justin and Patricia's choreography, Paul's costumes, Adam's production design, the hair, makeup, etc. . . . completely shine through that entire sequence.

ADAM STOCKHAUSEN (production designer): We looked at a lot of gyms. We had a series of requirements, because we had so many dancers that had to fit in the space. Yet we didn't want it to be gigantic. It had to be intimate enough to hold the dance but large enough to film in. It also needed a stage and an interesting space for the Sharks to come in, as their entrance into the dance is the big event. It needed to have bleachers, because Tony and María meet underneath them while the dance is taking place. All of this had to be built, and it had to be of a certain period. That took quite a bit of hunting.

JUSTIN PECK (choreographer): "Dance at the Gym" was a lot to choreograph and coordinate. On top of this, we had planned some incredibly ambitious camera shots (many extended one-ers, where the camera doesn't cut for a very long

Top
Rachel Zegler (María) and Josh Andrés Rivera (Chino)

Bottom
David Alvarez (Bernardo) and Ariana DeBose (Anita)

Opposite
María (Rachel Zegler), her date, Chino (Josh Andrés Rivera), and her watchful brother, Bernardo

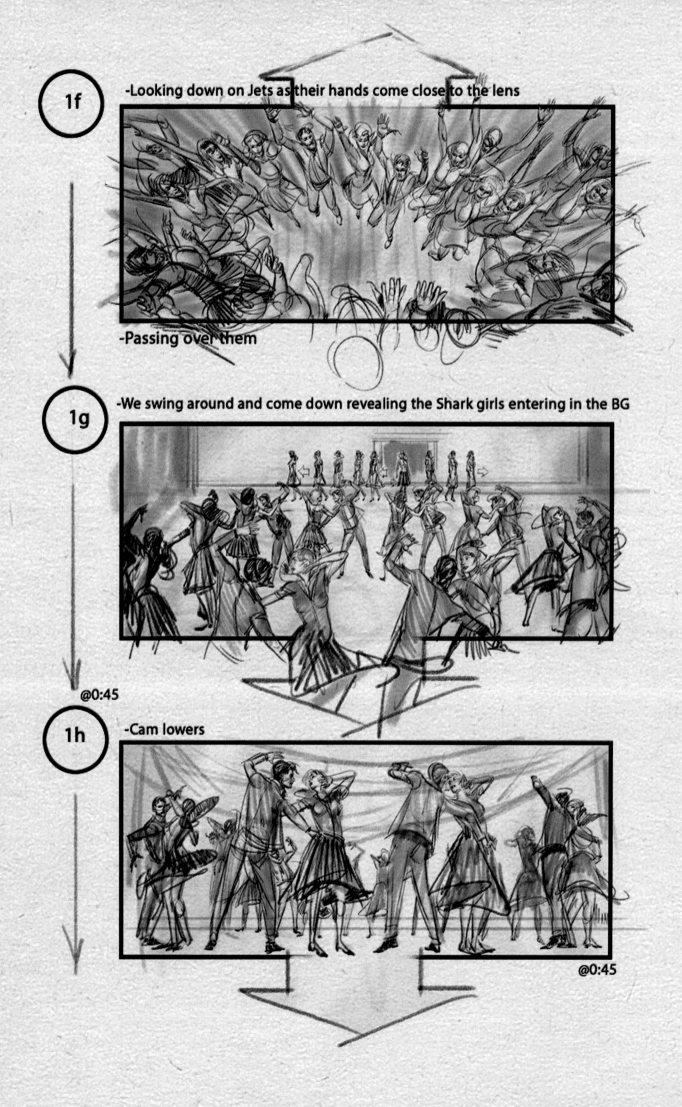

period of time). These shots involved many people, many moving parts, some very complex choreography, and a precision in timing. These were some of the most challenging moments of the film to capture. Because of that, any time that we printed one of these dynamic and energetic shots, it was met with a collective gratification. I remember Steven and I jumping up and high-fiving each other after capturing the opening extended shot of "Dance at the Gym."

PATRICIA DELGADO (associate choreographer): "Dance at the Gym" had to first be experienced in the rehearsal room; Justin and Steven together with the dancers finding their way. It was incredible to observe! They would place two extra-high ladders side by side and use Steven's iPhone to film the dancers from above. One challenge for the dancers was to learn how to not project too far out into the audience, like they are used to in a more traditional proscenium

arch stage. We also didn't exactly know where the "audience" would be. We had to think about the movement in a 360-degree manner so that no matter where the camera was, it would be capable of capturing a fully committed aspect of the movement! Onstage, we're used to projecting to the last row at the very top of the house, but here there was the possibility of a camera right there on a close-up of your face, so learning how to be subtle and natural in their expressions while dancing was also something we worked toward.

MATTHEW SULLIVAN (executive music producer/music supervisor): "Dance at the Gym" is composed of several very distinct segments; it starts off with the blues, and this big-band, brass-jazz piece going. That's called "Blues." This is where we come across and start meeting our characters. The Sharks are coming in, the Jets are already dancing, and they start to get into a bit of a fight. That's when "Blues"

Opposite
Storyboards by Raymond Prado

Above
Concept art of the Promenade by Hugh Sicotte

ends. You have "Promenade," which is the circle dance where you have boys to the left, girls to the right. They're spinning around, and they stop, and they're looking at each other and they're all matched up—Sharks girls with Jets guys, Jets guys against Sharks girls, and then we have a great moment, which is new to this movie, with Anita telling the band to spice it up a little bit and play the "Mambo." The "Mambo" kicks in, with Wayne Bergeron, who is one of the best trumpet players in the world. We extended his trumpet solo so he has more time to really blare and hit some high notes. To me, it's probably the best version of "Mambo" that exists. We also brought in a bunch of Puerto Rican musicians from New York, for some real authentic Puerto Rican flavor.

Gustavo Dudamel worked with them to get the backbeat, the heart of the song, to feel authentic and as Puerto Rican as possible. During the trumpet solo, Tony and María see each other from across the gym. They go in the back behind the bleachers and they start the "Cha-Cha," which is a little bit of a ballet dance; that moment really sums up this instant love connection that they have. And then during their dialogue there's a piece of music called "The Meeting Scene," which underscores their first conversation. Coming out of this, we have "Promenade Reprise," which is a slow version of the piece we heard earlier in the sequence. It's abruptly stopped when Bernardo finds María and Tony underneath the bleachers, and we have a little bebop song called "Jump,"

which now has the kids on the floor having a dance with dialogue of Bernardo versus Tony.

MICHAEL KAHN (editor): One of the big things I do on Steven's movies is build a temp music track, before the real score goes in. This was a very different situation, because we already had the music. And Steven wanted to be extremely respectful of the original composition. So we had to be careful each time we made a picture change, an edit—in fact, Sarah Broshar, who works with me, was very influential in making sure we never betrayed the music.

SARAH BROSHAR (editor): There's so much energy in the choreography and

in the camera movements, and such great performances. We had a cut of it done, but we kept looking at all of the different takes; we had so many choices, so many different angles and performances. . . . We were so impressed with the actors and how many times they would perform each take. . . . You literally felt exhausted for them, just watching the dailies! Yet, in the final edited version, it appears so effortless and seamless.

ADAM STOCKHAUSEN: When we were looking at the surfaces and the finishes of things, it was something that we were doing together with Justin and the whole choreography team. We would have these giant

The Sharks dance the "Mambo" and the Jets dance the "Blues."

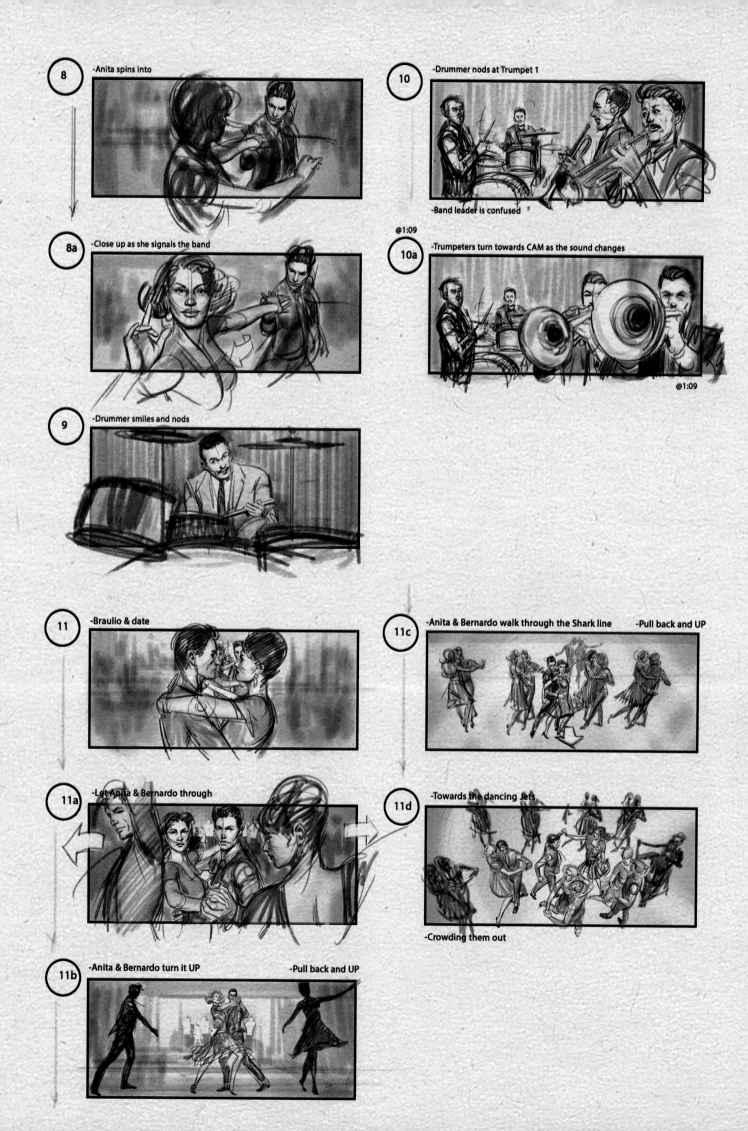

8 -Anita spins into

8a -Close up as she signals the band

9 -Drummer smiles and nods

10 -Drummer nods at Trumpet 1

-Band leader is confused

@1:09

10a -Trumpeters turn towards CAM as the sound changes

@1:09

11 -Braulio & date

11a -Let Anita & Bernardo through

11b -Anita & Bernardo turn it UP   -Pull back and UP

11c -Anita & Bernardo walk through the Shark line   -Pull back and UP

11d -Towards the dancing Jets

-Crowding them out

11e -CAM lowers as we dolly back with Anita & Bernardo

11f -Anita & Bernardo dance in between Riff & Graziella

11g -Riff & Graziella separated

Storyboards by Raymond Prado

sample boards for the gym floor, and then we made large-format samples of those that they could dance on to get a sense of (a) was it going to work, and (b) what kind of treatments would they have to do to the shoes—would it be leather soled or rubber soled.

GARY RYDSTROM (re-recording mixer/ sound designer): Tod Maitland (on-set sound mixer) got the time to record the dancing actors passing by with the music playing only in their earpieces. That recording became a bed, a real basis for the dancing in this scene. We sweetened with Foley to make it bigger than life, but the key to this dance is that it's aggressive; it feels like a fight unto itself.

ARIANA DeBOSE (Anita): I do have the most beautiful, glorious costumes. Paul Tazewell, our costume designer, said, "We're going to do a black dress but with a red petticoat." I said: "Sign me up!"

PAUL TAZEWELL (costume designer): For Anita, I wanted to make choices for her clothing that were visually original from other productions that I have seen. I chose to dress her in black for "Dance at the Gym" because I wanted for it to cut a very strong silhouette against the sea of color within the gym. The surprise is when you see that her petticoat is red, suggesting her internal fire and exuberance.

ARIANA DeBOSE: I also loved working with Kay Georgiou and Judy Chin in the hair department, and our key makeup person, Mandy Bisesti, who came up with this cat-eye look that needed to appear like it was just a little too much. Steven had a lot to do with my hair. I was very clear that I wanted something that separated me from Rita Moreno in the original film and from Chita Rivera on Broadway. Steven wanted something that looked very young; initially my hair was a little longer, and we eventually cut it down so it would be all the same length around the back. And I think it was a good choice.

TALIA RYDER (Tessa): During production, we had one dress rehearsal in the space where we were going to film "Dance at the Gym." The first time we all saw each other in our costumes felt like Christmas morning. We all marveled at Paul [Tazewell]'s incredible work and, once we were all dressed, gave him a standing ovation for his beautiful creations. Rehearsing in the gym for the first time was surreal. Seeing everyone in costume in the space made the whole scene come to life in a way I hadn't experienced yet.

PATRICK HIGGINS (Baby John): Talia Ryder was my partner for "Dance at the Gym." She said to me, "I've never danced on film before." I told her I'd never danced on film either.

From left: Carlos Sánchez Falú (Pipo), Brian d'Arcy James (Officer Krupke), Rachel Zegler (María), Ariana DeBose (Anita), and David Alvarez (Bernardo)

But once we got in there, the costumes, just the atmosphere, made it click.

KRISTIE MACOSKO KRIEGER: From the start of rehearsals, the atmosphere among the cast was unlike any other I've experienced on a movie set. There was a mutual love and respect apparent in their interactions, and everyone became fast friends, and we quickly recognized that this was a once-in-a-lifetime experience for the actors. We wanted to make sure that everyone had an opportunity to document their experiences on set and brought a 1950s-style photo booth for the cast to use and have fun with in between takes. The photo booth was the perfect touch—it was a fun way to continue to foster those friendships, and it helped everyone get into character for this pivotal scene.

MADDIE ZIEGLER (Velma): What was really cool was that prior to us filming it in pieces, Steven had us do the number from beginning to end. And it was so helpful, because there were obvious challenges—for instance, wearing period costumes and shoes. The dresses were huge. I have more experience dancing barefoot, so I had to adjust a bit to be comfortable dancing in heels. I had scabs all over my feet from the shoes, but it didn't even matter—nothing could have gotten in the way of how excited I was to be filming a movie this big with the legend that is Steven Spielberg.

BRIAN D'ARCY JAMES (Officer Krupke): "Dance at the Gym" could be *the movie* as far as I'm concerned. Right before filming the scene in pieces, Steven and Justin just let the dancers do the whole number from beginning to end. To see it all just play out was breathtaking.

PALOMA GARCIA-LEE (Graziella): Mike Faist does love to immerse himself. I said to him, "I want to be dating when we're on set. I want to build a physical relationship, so when the camera's rolling, it doesn't look strange, it's not forced." I consider myself a pretty immersive and method actress, and little did I know, I was very much meeting my match with Mike. We would travel to work together and just really build this rapport. And you see that connection in "Dance at the Gym."

That was one of the hardest weeks I have ever worked in my life. And I just grew so much by keeping the dancing fresh and alive. . . . That experience was transformative. Graziella has more depth than in any previous productions; I've gotten to flex my acting muscles in a way that I've always wanted to, and this movie has given me the opportunity.

MIKE FAIST (Riff): We had a blast with one another, creating this toxic relationship that Riff and Graz have. It's that young love that is not great. I remember Paloma told me Graz

Previous page
Behind the camera: Steven Spielberg

Opposite
Mambo! David Alvarez (Bernardo) and Ariana DeBose (Anita)

would be with anyone who leads the Jets. But with Tony that was maybe a little bit harder for her character to let go.

EDRIZ E. ROSA PÉREZ (Jacinta): My parents are both Puerto Rican, but my dad is a singer, so you can imagine how excited he is about this project. And both my parents have always been so supportive of me.

   "Dance at the Gym" is the number that I auditioned with, so it was supposed to be the one that I was most familiar and comfortable with. But it was still a lot of pressure; it's the Sharks women's dance. We have to show that we're strong, confident women through the acting and still focus on the dance. I wanted to make sure I represented my women correctly!

ADRIEL FLETE (Julito): We filmed "Dance at the Gym" in Brooklyn, which happens to be my hometown. . . . This is the first movie I've ever done. I'm living the dream and living it on the grounds where I grew up!

ANA ISABELLE (Rosalía): On the first day my call time was at 4:15 A.M. And then we were dancing until 6:00 P.M., and our bodies start to shut down a little bit. But the amount of excitement and appreciation for this moment that we were living was so, so huge that hours passed and we just kept dancing. I was born and raised in Puerto Rico, and I've been living in the United States for maybe six, seven years. And having the opportunity to represent my people

in a Hollywood film is just amazing. I am so proud that Steven Spielberg and Tony Kushner, with his amazing script, are giving the message that we Puerto Ricans are Americans.

KEVIN CSOLAK (Diesel): My mom owns a dancing school, and at the end of the season we'd rehearse for the end-of-the-year showcase in the gym at our middle school. Every year for the past fifteen years I've been dancing in gyms, and being here, doing "Dance at the Gym," feels nostalgic.

DAVID ALVAREZ (Bernardo): This scene is a dance-off between Puerto Ricans and the Jets, who are Irish, Polish, Italians, and a mix of other cultures. Everyone is coming in to have fun, and all of a sudden it gets separated between Sharks and Jets. Everyone starts to show off their skills, their culture, how they dance, how they move, and there's a big difference in styles between Sharks and Jets.

ILDA MASON (Luz): There was the sense of community; I just felt like I could be free, and it was pure joy. It's also full of fire and has an important message about clashing points of view.

JUSTIN PECK: Stylistically, it was important to apply a different sense of movement to Bernardo and Anita compared to Riff and Graziella. They come from very different backgrounds, and their movement needed to reflect those influences. Additionally, this helped

Riff (Mike Faist) romances Graziella (Paloma Garcia-Lee).

to give each character their own unique identity through dance expression. For example, Anita is a very strong character who is constantly challenging Bernardo. This makes for an explosive chemistry between them, especially as they carve through the dance floor together. Riff, on the other hand, is more of a lone-wolf leader. He's more concerned with the bigger picture (especially how it all pertains to his gang) and is confident that his partner, Graziella, will always be by his side. These characteristics, all expressed through movement, guided me in shaping the choreography not only for the dance at the gym, but for the leadership and gang dynamics of these respective characters.

DAVID ALVAREZ: Every single person wanted to be there, and no one asked, "Are we done yet?" We were just in the moment, we were having fun, and when they would say, "That's a wrap for today," we just went, "Wow. . . . I guess it's back to normal life until tomorrow." There were moments when Steven would play back the scenes on the monitor. It would be all of us watching, clapping and cheering with him, giving everyone hugs.

JONALYN SAXER (Rhonda): I don't think I've ever worked with a group of people that has so immediately clicked. Normally you think, *Okay, I spent all my time at work with those people. I've got to go home*, but

we were all energized, and everyone was so supportive and positive that you just wanted to stick around. For a lot of us, this is our first movie, but we have worked on Broadway or in the ballet world together. It's great to be experiencing this with friends!

JANUSZ KAMINSKI (director of photography): Steven's strength comes from bringing out the best in you in every aspect, not just in terms of your work, but also how you carry yourself. Be proud and respectful and tolerant. We were making a movie about tension and the lack of tolerance, and so it became even more important for Steven to embrace everyone. Steven was invigorated by making this movie.

KYLE ALLEN (Balkan): It was brutal, very hot. I was melting. A lot of the guys get to take off their jackets at various points. . . . I was not one of those guys. It was both emotionally and physically exhausting. But unanimously, there's no place we would have rather been.

JANUSZ KAMINSKI: Every time you're dealing with a whole bunch of people in the frame, it's a big challenge for the cinematographer, because you're not able to have very precise lighting. Yet you need precise lighting, because there's a story being told. It's not just people dancing; it's a tension between two groups, there's romance happening, there's a competition.

Top
Graziella (Paloma Garcia-Lee) and Riff (Mike Faist) challenge Bernardo (David Alvarez) and Anita (Ariana DeBose) on the dance floor.

Bottom
Steven Spielberg frames a shot, alongside Justin Peck, 2nd assistant Connie Huang, Steadicam operator John "Buzz" Moyer, and A camera operator Mitch Dubin.

-Riff takes Graziella & heads back to dance floor

-Couples follow Riff & Graziella, who looks back at Tony
-Tony greeeted by other Jet couples

2

-Wide   -Behind Tony   -Maria & Chino in BG w/ Sharks

-Jets greet Tony & run to join Riff and Graziella on Dance Floor

3

-Tony looks back at Dance Floor as his friends exit

-Blurred dancers in FG

Storyboards by Raymond Prado

As the cinematographer, you have to enhance those moments. You create tension through light, camera movement, composition. For the confrontation between the two groups, you want to separate those two groups and create two different environments in the lighting. It's not that one is dark and one is brighter. They both have certain brightness in the center, and the edges of the frame fall a bit darker. And when they connect, they go into another pool of light.

Because we're dealing with dancers, and many of them are in the frame, there's a mathematical formula that applies toward exposure and the so-called f-stop. The higher the f-stop, the sharper the image; the lower the f-stop, the secondary row of dancers will go very quickly out of focus. If you shoot at heavy stop —eight or eleven—then you have a deep focus; you can maintain sharpness for all the participants in the frame. And that requires a tremendous amount of light. There's nothing worse than seeing dancers go out of focus as they're traveling through the space. This was a movie that had to be sharp all the way from the foreground to the background to reflect the beauty of the story, to reflect the beauty of the dance.

JUSTIN PECK: The "Mambo" section of "Dance at the Gym" is where we really see the Jets and the Sharks dancing full throttle in competition with each other. There's an intense game taking place where each gang tries to one-up the other. In the midst of this tumult is when we start to notice Tony and María locking eyes. There's a kind of indescribable attraction that is permeating between the two of them, which we get to witness in real time. They slowly slip away and disappear underneath the bleachers to have their first interaction, which we think is going to be a conversation but is actually a very intimate dance. Personally, I am always fascinated by how much can be communicated without words. This first moment between Tony and María was just so gratifying to explore the dance language of, especially once we were on set and I was able to see what Steven was capturing through the lens.

ANSEL ELGORT (Tony): I was jealous at "Dance at the Gym." . . . I wanted to dance with them all. But I had to go be brooding Tony, who's not in the mood to dance until suddenly, there is María. . . .

PAUL TAZEWELL: The first choice that Steven requested for María was that she appear in an iconic white dress for "Dance at the Gym." It is the first time that Tony ever sees her, and for him she represents innocence, light, freshness, and a new life of possibility.

RACHEL ZEGLER (María): The scene under the bleachers was my first day of filming. We were supposed to shoot this later on, but the

Previous page
Tony (Ansel Elgort) spots María on the dance floor.

Opposite
Storyboards by Raymond Prado

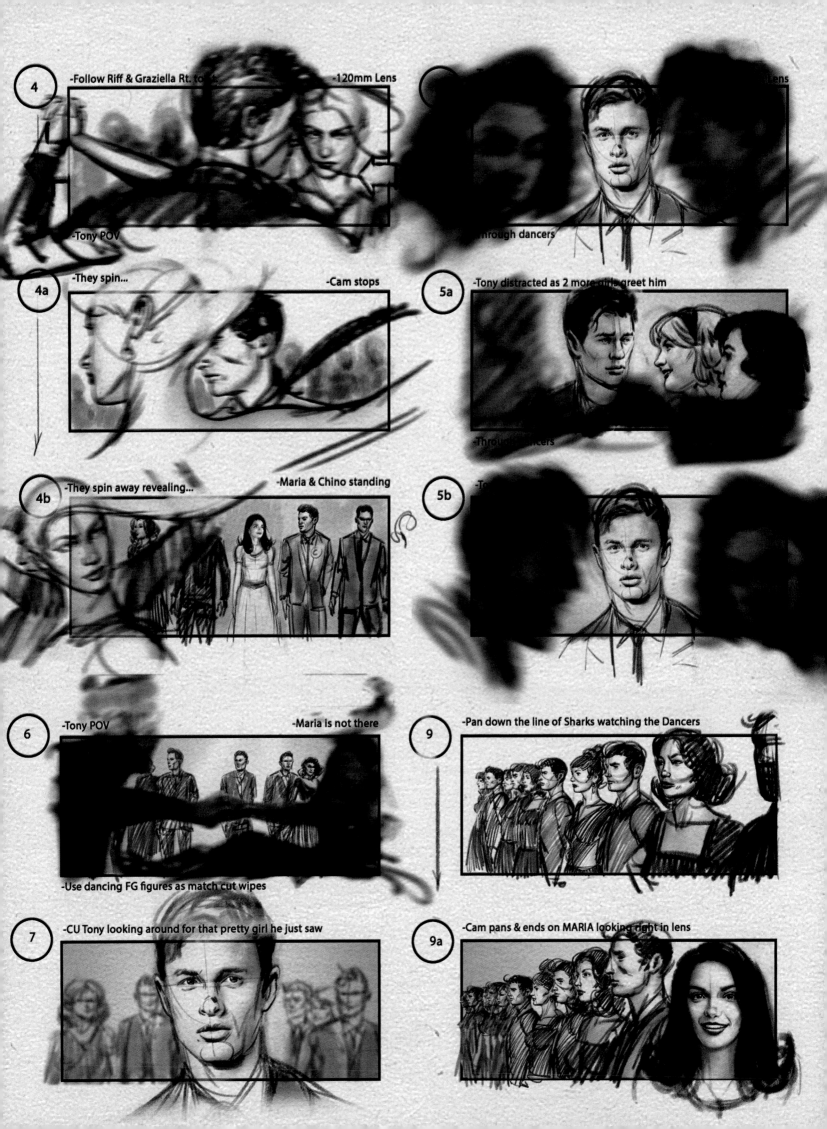

4 -Follow Riff & Graziella Rt. to... -120mm Lens

-Tony POV

...hrough dancers

4a -They spin... -Cam stops

5a -Tony distracted as 2 more girls greet him

-Through dancers

4b -They spin away revealing... -Maria & Chino standing

5b -To...

6 -Tony POV -Maria is not there

-Use dancing FG figures as match cut wipes

9 -Pan down the line of Sharks watching the Dancers

7 -CU Tony looking around for that pretty girl he just saw

9a -Cam pans & ends on MARIA looking right in lens

Maria (Rachel Zegler) and Tony (Ansel Elgort): love at first sight . . .

schedule changed due to bad weather and I got a call the night before. I was like, *Here we go. . . . This is it.* I was incredibly nervous. I remember telling Ansel this felt like the day of my first screen test.

ANSEL ELGORT: Rachel is a prodigy. Some people are born with it. And she has become one with music and one with being a performer since she was a kid just parading around her bedroom, listening to musicals. It seems effortless for her. This is her first job, just turned eighteen, easy breezy. She's laughing and joking around before every take, and all of a sudden, she turns it on.

TONY KUSHNER (screenwriter/executive producer): We were on location, filming the war council scene in the boys' bathroom, and I noticed that Adam Stockhausen had used the same tile both in the bathroom and in the morgue where Anita sees the bodies of Bernardo and Riff. Adam connected the beginning of the rumble with its horrific conclusion. It's subtle and subliminal and true to the tragic nature of this tale: None of this destruction was unknowable or unpreventable.

Bernardo (David Alvarez) gets between María (Rachel Zegler) and Tony (Ansel Elgort).

"MARÍA"

```
EXT. A BASKETBALL COURT - NIGHT

The basketball court is enclosed by the school and
a high fence. Tony's outside, clutching the fence,
staring in at the empty court. He gives it a fierce
shake and hangs from it, pressing against it. He
closes his eyes and quietly calls:

TONY

María . . .

—from the script by Tony Kushner
```

STEVEN SPIELBERG (director/producer): Tony's a tricky character. He needs to be a tough gutter rat, but then look at what he sings: He has to be someone really capable of love and unashamed to wear his heart on his sleeve. We looked for a year for Tony, then Ansel came in. Sometimes on camera he looks even younger than he is, then in the next second he looks like Marlon Brando. He has great power, and also vulnerability. He is boy and man and so facile at how often these qualities are interchangeable. Ansel found a way to create a Tony who's emerging from the shadows, struggling hard to find the light, which is his natural element—which makes what happens to him all the more devastating.

ANSEL ELGORT (Tony): "María" is a hard song. Leonard Bernstein wrote it like an opera, and I hadn't sung opera in a long time. I started working with an opera coach; we did hours of vocal exercises and sang "María," phrase by phrase, for months. During the long period of the audition process, I was able to continue working on it until I could convince Steven that I could sing it.

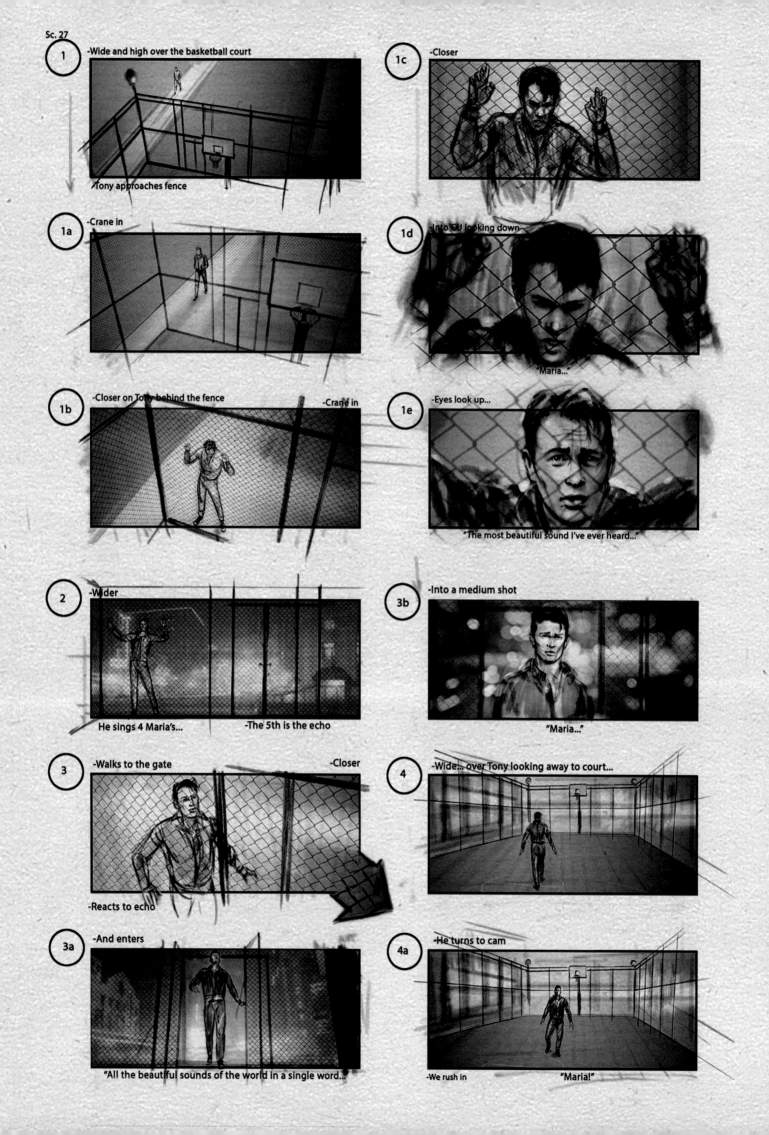

Sc. 27

1 -Wide and high over the basketball court

-Tony approaches fence

1a -Crane in

1b -Closer on Tony behind the fence

-Crane in

2 -Wider

He sings 4 Maria's...   -The 5th is the echo

3 -Walks to the gate   -Closer

-Reacts to echo

3a -And enters

"All the beautiful sounds of the world in a single word..."

1c -Closer

1d -Into CU looking down

"Maria..."

1e -Eyes look up...

"The most beautiful sound I've ever heard..."

3b -Into a medium shot

"Maria..."

4 -Wide... over Tony looking away to court...

4a -He turns to cam

-We rush in   "Maria!"

GUSTAVO DUDAMEL (conductor): Every single part of *West Side Story* is beautiful, but I can say my favorite is "María" because the love of my life, my wife, is named María.

ADAM STOCKHAUSEN (production designer): We have a playground with the Puerto Rican mural, and then we have the long fenced playground Tony goes into for the "María" number, and lots of other fences throughout the film. The most challenging aspect about finding those locations is the campaign to plant trees in New York City; when you look back at the reference from the fifties and earlier, there weren't that many trees on the streets. The biggest thing was finding schoolyards or playground areas that weren't surrounded by a wall of green trees and where you could actually see depth and the neighborhood.

ROBERT STRIEM (supervising location manager): This film is very unique in that it gave us the opportunity to engage in communities in an immersive way. A great example would be María's alley, where we had three scheduled days, two of them overnight, filming in the alley behind an entire square block of buildings in Washington Heights. We literally got to know everyone who lived there, made arrangements with all of them—whether it was hanging curtains, placing a light, putting an actor in the window, putting someone on their fire escape. The goal was to involve everyone, and it worked out.

ANSEL ELGORT: I sing "María" over short sections. . . . I'm climbing over a fence or I'm running down the alley; the song takes Tony throughout the city on this journey of discovery. It starts internally and then he decides, *I've got to find her.* He is yelling for María because he thinks this might be her neighborhood. He almost gives up hope, and just by chance, there she is.

MATTHEW SULLIVAN (executive music producer/music supervisor): As a whole, the music in *West Side Story* is very well set. But we can take every song and adjust the tempo, work from the performance of the actors, and also change the key to help suit the actors' vocals. Let's just take the example of "María." We moved it to a different key for Ansel's vocal abilities and for his range. We actually have a new musical intro for it, and all was approved by the Bernstein Estate and Stephen Sondheim. For every musical, you'd love to do it all live, but many times you're not allowed to do that for a variety of reasons: the set noise, for instance. And for "María," Tony is going from one location to another, and each place had its own texture. So we did that number to playback—yet we also recorded it live, and sometimes we've been able to use a little bit of the live performance, mixed in with the prerecorded one.

Previous spread, left; opposite
Storyboards by Raymond Prado

Previous spread, right
Tony (Ansel Elgort) scales fire escapes for a secret rendezvous with María (Rachel Zegler).

Clockwise from top left
Ansel Elgort as Tony; Steven Spielberg checks a shot; from left: 1st assistant A camera operator Mark Spath, 2nd assistant A camera operator Connie Huang, Ansel Elgort, and Rachel Zegler (María)

Ansel Elgort (Tony) and Rachel Zegler (María)

"TONIGHT"

Tony reaches the railing of María's fire escape. He
grabs hold of an iron brace holding up her landing,
and, his feet on the railing, he cantilevers himself
as far out as his arm extends. María, terrified and
thrilled, reaches down to him, laughing as she sings.
—from the script by Tony Kushner

ADAM STOCKHAUSEN (production designer): We built sets in a
warehouse at Steiner Studios, not on a proper stage. That warehouse is very tall,
and that worked great for "Tonight," where Tony is climbing up the fire escape. For
the beginning of the number, we first went to a real alley and filmed Tony walking
up to María's building. That way, we set it in reality, but it wasn't practical to film
the rest on location.

ANSEL ELGORT (Tony): For the song "Tonight," I kept pleading, "Please don't
put a harness on me, I can climb it, just put a big pad in case I fall." They did put a
harness on me anyway, but I do like that there's danger that comes along with the
song. Tony is almost teasing María with the danger of falling from the fire escape.

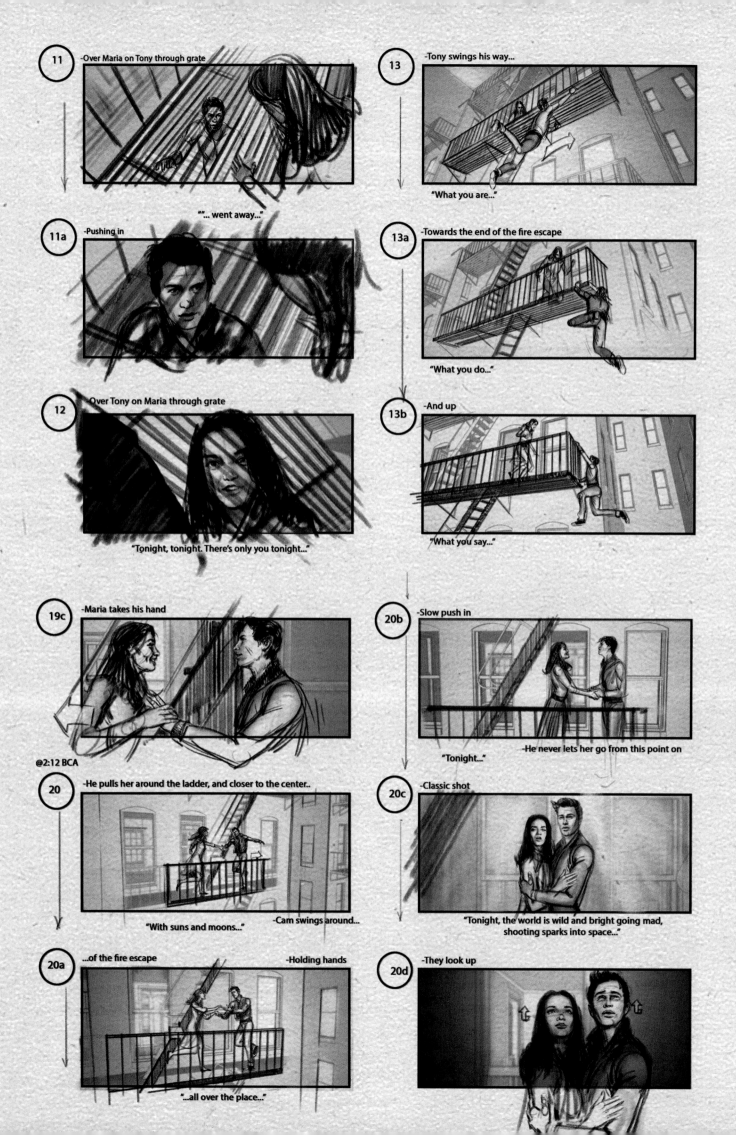

RACHEL ZEGLER (María): The balcony song was a big part of my audition process from the very beginning, and it was also last thing I shot. It really felt so emotional and holds the charm of Shakespeare's *Romeo and Juliet*.

```
     Tony lowers himself to
the ground. He looks up,
and María's leaning over
the railing, watching.
They wave. He walks away,
then turns for one last
look. They wave again, and
she disappears. He turns
and disappears into the
darkness.
     —from the script by
Tony Kushner
```

Opposite
Storyboards by Raymond Prado

This page
Concept art by Alexios Chrysikos

"AMERICA"

("America" begins:) The alley outside Anita's and Bernardo's bedroom. Clotheslines strung between pulleys are being reeled, laundry is being clothes pinned in time to the opening beats of the song. There's a whole community waking up, women are doing laundry, people having coffee, reading papers, kids playing.
　　—from the script by Tony Kushner

STEVEN SPIELBERG (director/producer): In the Broadway musical and in the Robert Wise film, "America" is done on a rooftop at night. We decided to bring "America" out on the street, in the morning, and it involves the entire Puerto Rican neighborhood. By the end of it, we have what is known as *pachanga* [a Caribbean dance style with origins in Cuba], with hundreds of dancers joining the number. We filmed it in bright daylight, and over several neighborhoods.

ADAM STOCKHAUSEN (production designer): "America" goes to a lot of different places, and it was a big enterprise; it starts off in Bernardo, Anita, and María's apartment, but then it travels through the entire neighborhood. And so we had a series of large street sets. We did a piece of it in Paterson, but we also had a street corner on St. Nicholas Avenue in Harlem. We added signage; we painted a lot of buildings where facades had been sandblasted and cleaned. We tried as much as we could to bring them back down, to have a little bit more dirt and grime, as they would have been in the late 1950s.

Sc. 35

9

-Anita and sus amigas(dos) on stoop

-EXT. STOOP

-Walking down the steps

-Anita sings

9a

-Pull back with Anita

"I like to be in America!"

9b

-To next stoop as three more girls join and sing

-And surround Anita   "OK by me in America!"

This page
Storyboards by Raymond Prado

Opposite
From left: Ilda Mason (Luz), Ariana DeBose (Anita), and Ana Isabelle (Rosalía)

Beginning at Anita and Bernardo's apartment and spilling out onto the city streets, "America" was filmed in numerous locations across New York City and Paterson, New Jersey.

RENA DeANGELO (set decorator): While we were prepping, and for months, we were on a massive search for period garbage cans. We went to Brimfield, of course, the famous giant flea market up in New England. We had calls out to everybody we know, junk dealers, and we probably ended up purchasing two hundred garbage cans. But we also spent four weeks changing out windows, awnings, putting up signs, dressing all the storefronts, until it was time to film. Seeing the same neighborhood filled with period cars, buses, and extras just transported me to 1957.

TOD MAITLAND (sound mixer): We did prerecords before we started filming, and we play them back into earpieces when we film a scene. We do a few takes to playback; the actors get into it, and then we switch over to live recording.

It's always an added challenge when you're on location; there's so much activity going on at one time that it creates issues for recording dialogue, but it also creates a very rich tapestry of sounds. My boom operator, Mike Scott, and utility sound technician, Jerry Yuen, put microphones all over the place; that way, we can capture cars and cranes and everything else that's going on while we're doing dialogue. This is a very complex film, and I had to build a special cart to accommodate all of the different aspects of the recording. It was very important for Steven to have it all sound very real and gritty. Later on, re-recording mixer/sound designer Gary Rydstrom and re-recording mixer

Andy Nelson worked on bringing all of those elements together.

GARY RYDSTROM (re-recording mixer/ sound designer): Leading to "America," it was important to set up the neighborhood that Anita and María live in, and it's less about the traffic here than it is about the people and the activity—the clotheslines, the flapping clothing and the sweeping up and the kids playing. And we have a lot of Spanish-language voice recordings of Puerto Rican neighborhoods in New York to give it that authenticity. During the number, we have a fun aggression here with the women doing a lot of radical flapping of their dresses; we really accentuated the cloth flaps, because it felt like a statement in the way that the men dance versus the way the women do.

SARAH BROSHAR (editor): The non-musical sequences were very similar to editing any other dramatic films, but with the musical pieces, if you have a character singing on-screen, then the performance is locked into the timing of the song; and if you have to make a cut from, let's say, a close-up to a wide shot, you really have to make sure the transition with the song is not abrupt, or takes you out of the moment. And sometimes, we would ask ourselves, how fast do you get out of a song after it's over? Do you let the reality breathe in, and you let the dramatic world come in for a beat, or do you cut right out to the next scene? Those were interesting choices and decisions to make.

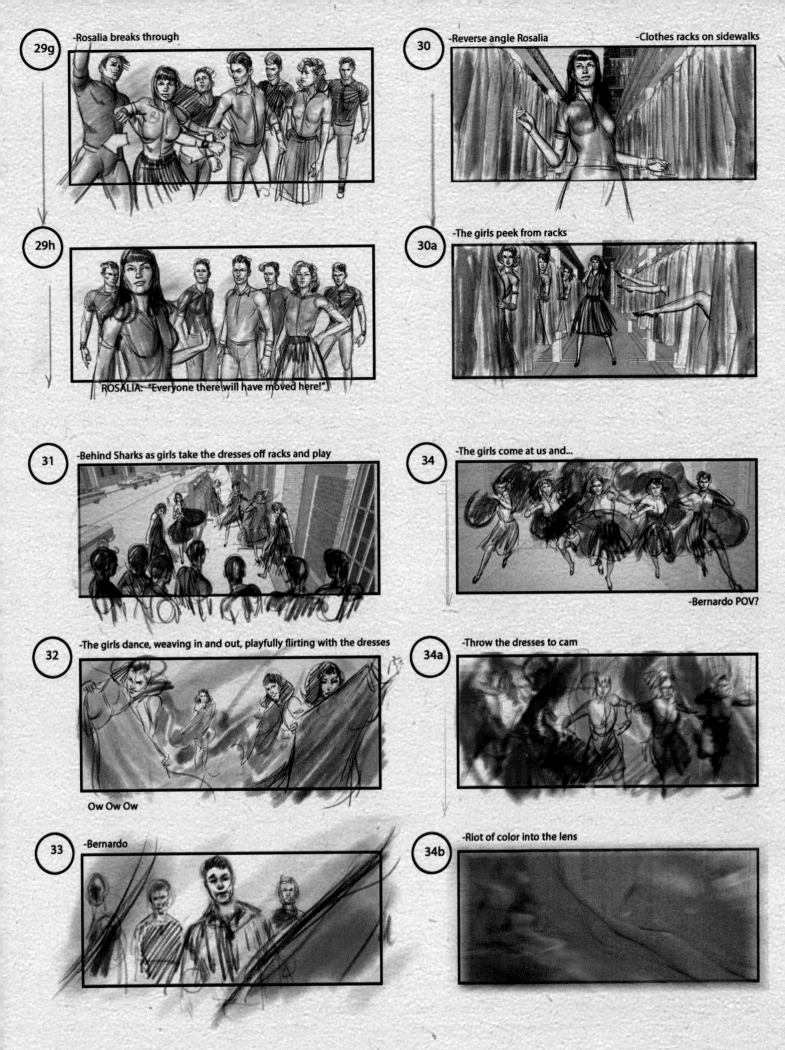

29g -Rosalia breaks through

29h ROSALIA: "Everyone there will have moved here!"

30 -Reverse angle Rosalia   -Clothes racks on sidewalks

30a -The girls peek from racks

31 -Behind Sharks as girls take the dresses off racks and play

32 -The girls dance, weaving in and out, playfully flirting with the dresses

Ow Ow Ow

33 -Bernardo

34 -The girls come at us and...

-Bernardo POV?

34a -Throw the dresses to cam

34b -Riot of color into the lens

Opposite
A playful moment in "America"

This page
Storyboards by Raymond Prado

STEVEN SPIELBERG: "America" is a joyful, funny, and sexy song, but at its heart it's a debate between two groups of Puerto Ricans: those who, like Anita, feel that they've found in New York a great place to realize their dreams; and those like Bernardo who are disillusioned by the racism and barriers to economic advancement they encounter every day. The creators of *West Side Story* were obviously aware of and sympathetic to this fierce division—as the children and grandchildren of Jewish immigrants, they certainly recognized a tormented relationship with both the old country and the new world.

KRISTIE MACOSKO KRIEGER (producer): "America" presents a complicated argument for many Puerto Ricans who struggle with Anita's disparagement of the island. The dialogue between Anita and Bernardo really communicates the challenges that many in the Puerto Rican and Latinx communities have experienced when coming to this country. This number alone will hopefully further contribute to important conversations around migration. But "America" also serves as a celebration of Anita and Bernardo's Nuyorican culture as a whole. During filming, some of our Sharks brought their family from Puerto Rico to set. They shared their personal stories—and you

13c -Pushing into Anita pointing to terrace Apt. on sign...

"I'l get a terrace apartment..."

-Still pushing in

13d -Bernardo's head pops up from behind sign   -Anita reacts

"Beter get rid of your accent!"

13e -He jumps over sign   -Girls exit left

Opposite
On the streets of New York filming "America"

This page
Storyboards by Raymond Prado

Previous spread
The Sharks men and women carry on a debate as they traverse the city, from the boxing gym to the streets.

14 -Bernardo is joined by his guys

14a -We follow the girls around the corner

14b -And they turn and keep walking backwards

"Life can be bright in America!"

could tell how emotional it was for them. Those visits were truly eye-opening for me, as they reinforced the importance of what the message of this film is all about.

ARIANA DeBOSE (Anita): "America" is all about perspectives, and it's beautiful to show who these two people are, and their love story in the context of the world they live in. They are on two very different sides. Anita is very much of the mindset that she is not going back to Puerto Rico, where there's no opportunity for her. She will always love home, but there's nothing there for her anymore. Bernardo thinks that things are better there. In many ways, Anita is a woman ahead of her time, and that really is a big part of her conflict with Bernardo.

ANDREI CHAGAS (Jochi): "America" was very special to all of us. When we started filming it, I don't think we really understood the magnitude of it. It was so big; it was beyond us.

CARLOS E. GONZALES (Chucho): We had just done a shot, and when we turned around, the music came on, and my mom, who was visiting the set, was bawling. Then we all started crying. My mom and my father left Cuba and brought me here to America when I was eleven. The whole reason I do what I do is to make their sacrifice worth it; they created the opportunity for me. To be able to have my mom on set and share those moments brings us full circle.

JULIAN ELIA (Tiger): David Bean, who played Tiger in the Robert Wise film, has a cameo in this new version. He is the owner of a fabric shop in the number "America." Meeting him was really thrilling. He explained how the film affected him for the rest of his life—his cameo proved it. He said, "*West Side Story* is a classic, and you are yourself part of it now—and that will change your life forever, just like it changed mine."

MYLES ERLICK (Snowboy): Like the other Jets, Snowboy is a lost soul. He's damaged, he had a crazy childhood, and his only family is the Jets. I grew up watching the original film, and it inspired me to want to dance. This new film will stand on its own. One thing that the production did that was very helpful was to bring in cast members from the first film. I got to meet Bert Michaels, who played the original Snowboy. Like him, I do feel that this experience is going to be part of me for the rest of my life!

JUSTIN PECK (choreographer): By coincidence, whenever we shot "America," the temperature was always in the nineties range! So the New York City summer heat naturally became part of the storytelling of "America." Our aim was to showcase the power, importance, and pride of the Puerto Rican community. We wanted to show how Bernardo and Anita move through their local neighborhood, interacting with their friends, neighbors, local business owners. These

Opposite
Storyboards by Raymond Prado

interactions become fodder for the bursts of dance that catch fire throughout the song. This was a very ambitious number with challenging transitions from one section to the next. It starts with just Bernardo and Anita in their apartment. They flow out onto their street, and it continues to slowly build in scale. Finally, "America" culminates in a massive block party at a major street intersection, with the entire community dancing a great *pachanga*. To me, the final moment of "America" feels like the closest ode to a classic Golden Age Hollywood musical in our film.

Part of the challenge with this number was the fact that we had to shoot on so many different locations, spread out among many unconnected days throughout our shoot schedule. Our goal was to maintain the consistency of the five-minute number despite the fact that it was actually shot over ten days or so, everywhere from Harlem to Paterson, New Jersey, to Queens.

ARIANA DEBOSE: Jeanine Tesori was very influential in helping Anita find her voice. I wanted to make the attempt to not sound like a pop star or a musical theater star. I wanted it to be imperfect. She and I found our way into understanding what that meant. Ultimately there's a freedom in her voice. The sound might be unconventional, but it's honest and authentic. As far as the dancing, Justin Peck has a very specific style, which I will confess is very hard to conjure on concrete streets! But it's beautiful and it's human, which is the common denominator among all of the

From left: choreographer Justin Peck, associate choreographers Patricia Delgado and Craig Salstein, Steven Spielberg, Ilda Mason (Luz), Ariana DeBose (Anita), and Ana Isabelle (Rosalía)

different facets of this team. We've been trying to create a story of humanity and everything that makes us human.

DAVID ALVAREZ (Bernardo): I remember both the sun and the lights were hitting us. Plus, I had this wool shirt that was thick and itchy, but it looked good. On the third day, the heat got so bad that we had to cancel filming. But the costumes all tell a little bit about who we are as characters. They had to be realistic. The last thing you want is the audience feeling they're seeing "Broadway costumes." Filming on the streets changed the whole experience, from the experience we'd had rehearsing at a dancing studio. You see people looking outside their windows, and you can feel that energy.

ADRIEL FLETE (Julito): My costume was wool, and it stretches. I was rigged into it with suspenders underneath that went through the shirt. But it looked good on the outside.

The energy in "America" spirals like a tornado when the music comes on, and it had a dynamic impact on the group. We all felt it; we all totally dove into it. We were creating the magic that Steven felt when he first watched *West Side Story*, but for a new era.

JANUSZ KAMINSKI (director of photography): While we were filming "America," one of the biggest challenges was to maintain a continuity with the visual storytelling. It's rather difficult to go on the brightly lit street at noon, with hot, harsh light, having many dancers, and making it glossy. We had to move fast to maintain the beauty of the dance, and the brightness of the colors. Anybody who knows a little bit about photography knows that if you have a bright top light, you get big shadows on people's faces. You end up bringing many big lights to compensate, and all of a sudden, you've got 100-degree weather, and lights that increase the temperature to 120; you've got dancers in full costumes. You can't be selfish and just think of your image; you also have to create a comfortable environment for the cast.

SARAH BROSHAR: "America" and the "Quintet" were interesting because they were basically shot over the entire production. Those were fun to see unfold as [editor] Michael Kahn and I kept getting new little pieces practically every week. We had the audio of the songs laid out, and as the film progressed, we'd fill out a hole and place shots, here and there. It wasn't really until the end of production that we could actually look at both "America" and the "Quintet" as a whole, and start finessing them.

RICKY UBEDA (Flaco): Altogether we rehearsed "America" for ten weeks. It's scary because you don't want to mess up a take, but you also want to make sure you're at your best in the take that will eventually end up in the film.

JULIETTE FELICIANO (Cuca):
The Shark women are empowered. They are fearless. It's about being here, standing our ground and speaking up. "America" embraces this sentiment. It's not just happy people dancing on the streets. It's about wanting to live our dreams here, in America.

DAVID ALVAREZ: The whole point of ending "America" with a kiss between Bernardo and Anita is to represent that no matter how differently they view this world, that kiss brings them together.

Top
Ariana DeBose (Anita)

Bottom
From left: executive producer/first assistant director Adam Somner, Steven Spielberg

Opposite
Bernardo (David Alvarez) and Anita celebrate their love at the end of "America."

Previous spread, top left
Bernardo (David Alvarez) and Anita (Ariana DeBose) are the center of attention as the street fills with dancers.

Previous spread, bottom left
"America" concept art by Alexios Chrysikos

Previous spread, right
David Alvarez (Bernardo) and Ariana DeBose (Anita) take direction from Steven Spielberg outside the boxing gym.

"GEE, OFFICER KRUPKE"

Mouthpiece/Krupke hoists Diesel by the back of his collar. Balkan jumps up into the Day Sergeant's desk as Big Deal throws him a Patrolman's raincoat hanging on the wall. Balkan puts it on backwards, making a judge's robe, then sits as Snowboy rises behind him, holding a filthy mop over his head for a Magistrate's white wig. A-Rab grabs the two flagpoles with the American and NY State flags and holds them in his crossed arms, before the bench; his hands are free to be the court stenographer.

—from the script by Tony Kushner

TONY KUSHNER (screenwriter/executive producer): ""Gee, Officer Krupke" is a delirious melody and the lyrics are incredibly funny, but it's a song about children who have been abused, whose parents are drug addicts, who have been exposed to violence and crime their entire lives. These kids make fun of themselves and their circumstances, they all but beg us to laugh at them, even as they describe a machine cynically designed to achieve the opposite of its ostensible function: This system is meant to cure juvenile delinquency but, in fact, perpetuates it.

The difficulty is that it works so gloriously as a comic number; it becomes hard to hear that it's telling you a lot that you need to know about what made these kids into feral, racist thugs. I asked Jeanine Tesori if it'd be possible to get rid of the exuberant, pie-in-the-face, oom-pah-pah intro, and instead begin with the words of the first verse, which are a plea for attention—sardonic, but still they ask Krupke, and us, to listen. Jeanine sat down at the rehearsal room piano and tried it, but she played and sang it slowly, quietly, cautiously, turning it into a request. It sounded shocking, and exciting, a way to hear a familiar song anew.

ADAM STOCKHAUSEN (production designer): "Krupke" takes place in the 21st Precinct, instead of being out on the street as in the original film. The Jets take over, mocking the cops and destroying the place. We shot it in a church hall in Brooklyn. It was the perfect size and shape and had the right bones. We totally redid the floor, painted it, and built in the interrogation rooms on the sides.

BEN COOK (Mouthpiece): As with several of the other musical numbers, "Krupke" is presented in a different context in this film. Riff and a few of the Jets go to the docks to obtain a weapon for the rumble, and the other half are on their own and get brought in by the police to get questioned about where the rumble is going to happen. Through a series of events, the Jets are left in the precinct alone. Baby John is really scared he could go to jail or to Rikers, and the number starts off with us singing to him. I pretend to be Krupke, and Kevin, who plays Diesel, plays a delinquent. It's fun, but the underlying tone of the entire number is really sad and carries a lot of anger; it shows just how broken our system is and how these kids get passed off from one person to another—to shrinks, social workers—before they're just spit back out onto the street. It makes them feel worthless, whether they

Above
Director of photography Janusz Kaminski on the "Gee, Officer Krupke" set

Opposite
Production designer Adam Stockhausen and Steven Spielberg

realize it or not. It was interesting to play with the tone of the piece.

BRIAN D'ARCY JAMES (Officer Krupke): The costume had a big influence on me. There's something about putting on a uniform and losing your identity in it and becoming the representation of an idea. I joked with the costume designer that this was the easiest costume fitting ever, because it never changes. However, polyester is an unforgiving fabric, and I'm pretty sure I had the most uncomfortable version of it. Standing around in hot New York City summer heat with that getup on was challenging. As far as the number itself, you get a sense that Krupke wants to put his arms around these guys and give them a chance to do the right thing. Yet he has to do his job, keep them in line. He's riding that line, which I think is really a great illustration of who he is as a person. The number is still about thumbing your nose to authority, but what's interesting about this version is that Krupke has to extricate himself from the scene to allow the Jets to make fun of him. He eventually gets to come back and see all the damage they've done to the precinct.

JANUSZ KAMINSKI (director of photography): On many occasions, but especially with "Krupke," I felt like I was inside the musical. It was like a 3-D Broadway show

experience and a privilege to be part of it that way. "Krupke" is a good example of this, because it was very physical; it's got all the "gags" of Broadway. . . . And it was very easy to work with the dancers because you knew they would hit their marks. Lighting on a given scene is very specific, and you always have certain marks for actors to hit; but you often have to allow them a certain freedom. There's no such worry with dancers, because their movements already have to be extremely precise and coordinated. They have great discipline.

TONY KUSHNER: We all knew the morgue set Adam Stockhausen built was in the basement of the church-turned-police-station where we were filming "Krupke," and everybody made a trip downstairs to see it. This wasn't planned, but I think it had an effect on the way "Krupke" was filmed and performed. Death was under our feet the whole time.

Following spread, top
Concept art by Stephen Tappin

Following spread, bottom
Steven Spielberg sets the scene for "Gee, Officer Krupke."

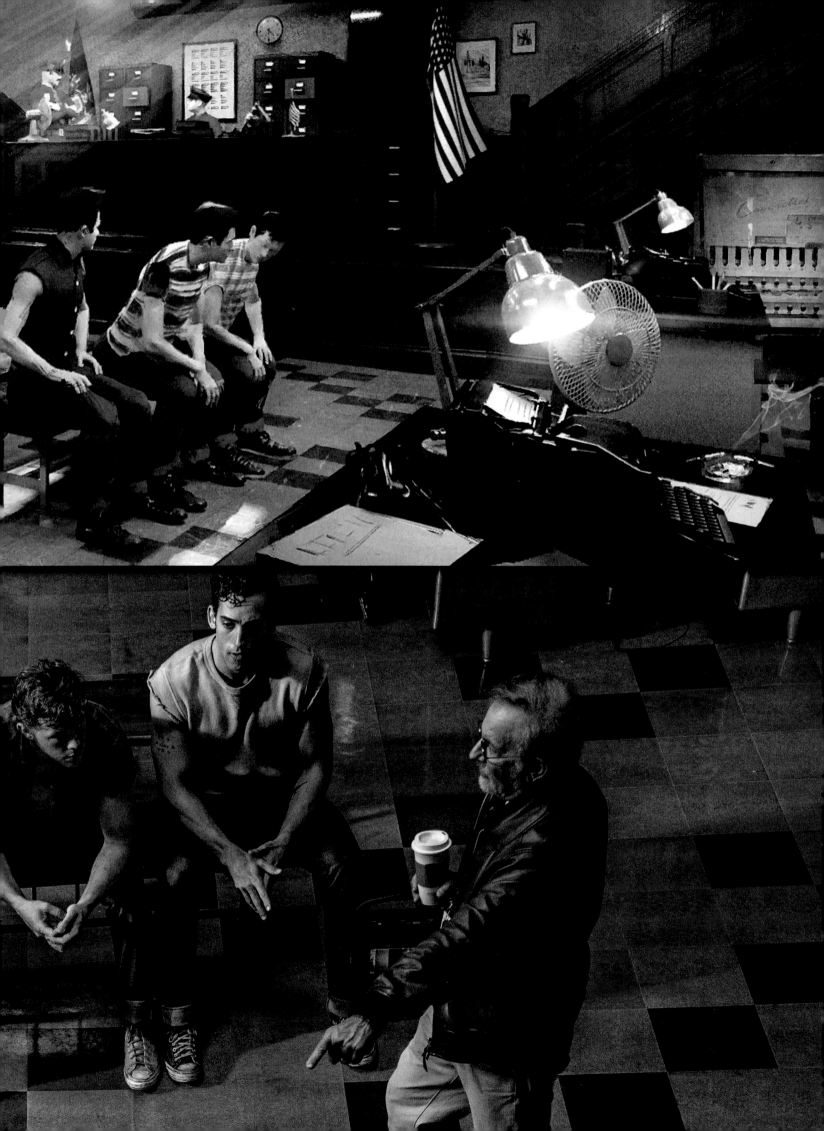

Opposite, top
The Jets wreak havoc in the precinct.

Opposite, bottom
Ezra Menas (Anybodys), Kevin Csolak (Diesel), John Michael Fiumara (Big Deal), Ben Cook (Mouthpiece), Myles Erlick (Snowboy), Patrick Higgins (Baby John), and stunt coordinator Mark Fichera on the set of "Gee, Officer Krupke"

Top
Steven Spielberg, Patrick Higgins, Jess LeProtto (A-Rab), executive producer/first assistant director Adam Somner, and Ezra Menas

Above
Kyle Allen (Balkan), Steven Spielberg, and Ben Cook

"ONE HAND, ONE HEART"

INT. THE GOTHIC CHAPEL IN THE CLOISTERS – AFTERNOON

María walks among the funerary figures on the sarcophagus lids. The afternoon sun sets stained glass windows ablaze.

She kneels in front of the four saints in the apse, crosses herself and prays. Tony stands near her.

—from the script by Tony Kushner

JEANINE TESORI (supervising vocal producer): When we shot "One Hand, One Heart," Rachel and Ansel sang it live, and I started weeping—the whole thing really hit me. I was very moved by the hard work and realized that people were not going to be able to see the process. The human voice to me is a miracle, and I was really overwhelmed by it.

ANSEL ELGORT (Tony): "One Hand, One Heart" is almost holy, a lullaby with two lovers on the exact same page, wanting to become one. It's the moment when Tony and María are saying vows to one another and promising that they're going to be together forever. It takes place in a crypt with a beautiful stained-glass window. We filmed the scene at the Met Cloisters in Washington Heights, New York. It's sung very softly in a way that could never be done onstage; you would need to project to the person in the last row, but here the audience is the camera. If it's a closeup, you can literally sing it as if you're talking. For this song, we only recorded it live; we didn't use playback.

RACHEL ZEGLER (María): We shot "One Hand, One Heart" twice. The first time was a sixteen-hour workday. It was exhausting. It was riveting. It was beautiful. But then Steven decided to revisit it and wanted new takes. It ended up being another long workday. We like to joke on set that "One Hand, One Heart" was a thirty-hour shoot. It's a very spiritual moment, especially because Tony doesn't seem to really believe in anything, while María is very devout. She wears her cross all the time. There's a cross over her bed. Spirituality is very important to the Latin culture and in Puerto Rico especially. But when we were at that specific location, it became very real because neither Ansel nor I had ever been there, just like Tony and María; there was a genuine sense of discovery for us.

JANUSZ KAMINSKI (director of photography): Steven had this really wonderful idea of Tony and María going into a little chapel and singing to each other. He wanted to create this effect by having a light behind a stained-glass window, moving up and down, and having very delicate light patterns across the actors' faces. But the final result was not as romantic, as warm as we wanted it to be. The colors were not popping through, so we reshot it with stronger colors, and relying on color gels rather than glass. We improved our technique of moving the light up and down, adjusting the exposure where the darker you go in the exposure, the more saturated the colors would be.

STEVEN SPIELBERG (director/ producer): With every single movie I've done with Janusz Kaminski, he finds something that I never knew I had, and he pulls it out of me. He is such a genius collaborator. I couldn't do this without him. And of course, he has an amazing crew, including our camera operator, Mitch Dubin, our focus puller, Mark Spath, our gaffer, Steve Ramsey, our Steadicam operator John "Buzz" Moyer, our key grip Mitch Lillian, and the on-set sound crew and everybody who works with him.

This page
Steven Spielberg and choreographer Justin Peck discuss the scene.

Opposite, top
Concept art by Stephen Tappin

Opposite, center
Steven Spielberg framing "One Hand, One Heart"

Opposite, bottom
Light streams through the windows of the chapel.

"COOL"

INT/EXT. DERELICT WAREHOUSE PIER - AFTERNOON

Sunbeams stream through huge gaps in the roof,
high above the crazily tilting floor. Startled birds
flap through the dusty air as the boys play cops and
robbers, duck behind rusty pillars, leap across holes,
the river 40 feet below.

Riff ducks behind a pillar. There's a tap on his
shoulder. He spins around, grinning, gun at the ready;
it's Tony. He puts his hand over Riff's gun and pushes
it down.

—from the script by Tony Kushner

STEVEN SPIELBERG (director/producer): We wanted the "Cool" dance
number to be really . . . cool and dangerous. In the original stage musical, it takes
place after the rumble, but in our film, it happens before. Riff has gotten a gun from
an Irish bar, and Tony is trying to get the Jets not to fight. He tries to get the gun
away from Riff, and they have a very stylized, existential dance, which the Robbins
estate saw and approved about four months before we started shooting.

We built a pier set over water with huge holes in it, with our guys having to
dance around them. For safety we put Plexiglas over every hole so nobody could
accidentally fall through.

A number like "Cool" was intimidating, but Justin Peck gave me the kind of
confidence I needed during rehearsals. He is not only collaborative but original
and uniquely inventive. He has no fear. When people see what Justin has done,

Tony (Ansel Elgort) wrenches the gun away from Riff (Mike Faist)
during "Cool."

they will see his art. I saw it on set, but when you see it cut together, it's an entirely different experience—"Cool" is one of the most original numbers I have seen in any musical.

JUSTIN PECK (choreographer): In terms of storytelling, choreography, setting, and style, "Cool" is one of the most bold and unique numbers in our film (especially when compared to the original). It is a high-reaching display, and because of that I was glad we started our shoot with this one.

I've done a lot of work in theater, and so because of that I am used to working within the parameters of the traditional theater proscenium stage. This process was much different. With "Cool," I was able to collaborate with Adam Stockhausen, our production designer, to create a fully customized environment for this number to take place. We were able to design every single detail, and created a kind of obstacle course of sorts for the number to move through.

Because the scenic possibilities were endless, it took a lot of effort and time to figure out. These parameters made for a complicated choreographic process. In order to fully figure this number out, I had to build up and break down the material at least three times before I had it right. But it was worth it. What we created is entirely designed for the film medium, and would not function properly in any other context.

We set and shot the number outdoors, on a dilapidated ferry terminal. It was exhilarating to be outdoors in such an epic location for the first time. We were battling the elements. Some days were bitter cold, and some very hot (the time of year in New York when the weather is turning from spring to summer). It rained on a couple of days and we had to reschedule some things. But we got it there, and finally wrapped what will be a very intense section of the film. It was the perfect kick-off to the journey ahead.

KRISTIE MACOSKO KRIEGER (producer): It was so much fun to see Steven and Justin Peck collaborate in real time on set. They worked so well together, and you could see how Steven truly has an eye for shooting dance sequences. Despite windy conditions that delayed shooting, our cast was so excited to dive into this number. The difficult choreography, stunts, and the intense playfighting were a lot for our actors to manage and balance, but their incredible work on those first few days came to life on camera; it really empowered us all and set the tone for the rest of the summer.

HARRISON COLL (Numbers): We'd seen computer renderings of the set, three-dimensional scale models, and pictures—but finally seeing it in person, it was hard to believe how much detail went into every barrel and

Top
Steven Spielberg's vision of "Cool" becomes a reality on the waterfront set.
Bottom
Steven Spielberg and choreographer Justin Peck

beam. It was a masterpiece that beautifully synthesized engineering with art and design. We immediately made ourselves at home in our new hideout habitat, treating it like our own personal playground. We took turns swinging on chains, running and sliding up and down ramps, and we even had a little chin-up competition. It was ideal for a bunch of rambunctious hooligans raring to fool around on the most spectacular jungle gym imaginable. Steven was understandably cautious and made sure to settle us with a serious safety talk. Eventually, we turned our attention to stepping through the choreography. We used our imagination with Justin's guidance to figure out how to organically and intuitively incorporate our surroundings into the dancing. It was electric. The danger felt real, and that brought life and authenticity to every step.

JEANINE TESORI (supervising vocal producer): Steven Spielberg turned and said, "This is like making an action movie." And it's really true. Activating a musical number is key. What are they doing? What does the song do? It's like a game of dominoes.

JUSTIN PECK: Ansel Elgort dances in our version of "Cool." In the original film, Tony doesn't dance much—only a little bit in "Dance at the Gym" with María, but usually Tony is mainly a singing part. We worked relentlessly with Ansel to take on the demands of this newly expanded version of Tony, which involved a great deal of training, coaching, and conditioning. He took it all in like a champ. And demonstrated that the dance language added a deeper layer to his character.

ANSEL ELGORT (Tony): We did "Cool" in a brand-new way. Riff gets all heated about giving up the gun, and Tony sings "Cool" to him. He lets him know that he's got to be cool. . . . And then it escalates into this dance on a pier that Justin Peck has choreographed and all kinds of action that Steven has added. There's dust being kicked as Tony and Riff are challenging each other. In the end, Riff gets the gun and runs off, and now Tony needs to go to the rumble to try to stop him from doing something fatal.

MIKE FAIST (Riff): Steven and Tony decided to make "Cool" about the relationship between Tony and Riff—we get to see the competition between them, the fallout and their breakup. With Justin, we just worked on it for hours at a time during rehearsals. That's where Justin's expertise and vision really came through; how do we dance while at the same time showing all the nuances that are happening between these two guys and showing where they're coming from, where they are now, and how they both don't really know how to move forward at the end of it. Crafting that was a very special time, for sure. Ansel and I worked on developing that

Opposite
From left: Mike Faist (Riff), Ansel Elgort (Tony), choreographer Justin Peck, 1st assistant A camera operator Mark Spath, associate choreographers Patricia Delgado and Craig Salstein, Steven Spielberg

relationship, a kind of openness and trust that is important because you're in an extremely vulnerable place . . . and you were really sharing pieces of yourself that are both ugly and beautiful.

HARRISON COLL: To me, cool means "defuse the anger." It means "keep it together." It's not necessarily about "being cool." It's about: 'Please relax, that tension is going to get you killed. We don't want a fight or something worse to happen.

Just try to play it cool and take the steam out of things. Easy does it."

PATRICIA DELGADO (associate choreographer): I remember for the entire week that we shot "Cool," Ansel and Mike would just jump up and down constantly. The crew would be setting up the lighting or adjusting something with the camera, and you would just see them deep in thought and staying in their character but still

moving their feet and bodies, if not in an intense way, at least in a light bounce, like a boxer during a boxing match. Their adrenaline was 100 percent on the entire time and their blood pumping not only for their physical bodies but for the emotional depth of this scene! They were so committed to making sure that it felt real.

ANSEL ELGORT: Janusz Kaminski's lighting is theatrical in itself. It is bright, drastic, and dramatic. In a scene like "Cool," there was sun coming from all directions; there was so much hard light on us, which made the scene that much more intense. We were sweating from all the light being pointed at us.

Working with Janusz is also great because he brings a humorous energy to the set. The way he's able to get his team to work very quickly and diligently to get the next shot ready is very unique and remarkable.

JANUSZ KAMINSKI (director of photography): Originally, I wanted to create water reflections on the faces of the actors. That was abandoned because we had sunny days, and we embraced the sun and used it to our advantage. The set was built in such a way that it almost looked like the rib cage of a whale; it was very skeleton-like. That created the opportunity for me to have shadows on the actors' faces as well as shadows on the ground to create tension.

Shadows give you tension, and when people go through shadows, it creates a kind of a staccato movement, and you feel a certain unease. For some reason, in today's cinema, cinematographers are afraid of shadows. But shadows are very important in this particular movie; they are part of the storytelling, part of the language, and this song created an opportunity for me to use them to create even more tension.

HARRISON COLL: Father's Day happened to fall on the last day of filming "Cool," the song I remember dancing to with my dad in my living room as a kid. My dad knew all the choreography, and we would dance the steps to the soundtrack or while watching the movie. He said he learned the steps from Jerry [Robbins]. I treasure that memory of dancing with my dad.

On the set that day, I seized the opportunity to memorialize my father. What better place to honor him than the set of Steven Spielberg's *West Side Story*. I brought a small picture of him, one of his old guayabera shirts, his watch, and a tin of his ashes, and I shared Father's Day with him. I felt him dancing with me. A feeling I will never forget.

After the last shot, when the crew began to close down the set, Justin, Patricia, Craig, Ansel, Mike, the other Jets, and I sat in a circle at the end of the pier to thank the universe for the past few days. We all said a little thank-you and took a couple of deep breaths. I took my dad's ashes from my jacket pocket and told everyone about him; who he was and how he was connected to *West Side Story* and how I felt that I needed to release him. I asked if they would help me by singing a verse from "Jet Song." We sang together, taking turns with each verse, starting with Mike singing "When you're a Jet you're a Jet all the way, from your first cigarette to your last dying day." While singing, we made our way over to this perfect little secluded beach that overlooked the harbor and the set perfectly. When we reached the end of the verse we screamed, "When you're a Jet you stay a Jet." With those words echoing into the atmosphere, the sun setting, and the wind blowing as if spirits were flying over our little hideout, I walked to the water, knelt down, and said, "I love you. Rest in peace." I threw the ashes into the air and watched as they flew over the entire set.

MIKE FAIST: Paul Tazewell worked with me in making unique choices in what Riff would wear. We worked on finding a bracelet and a necklace. The bracelet is actually Riff's mom's, and the necklace is an extra piece of jewelry that is based off of a photo I saw in a photography book by Bruce Davidson. Then there's Judy Chin and her work with the makeup. We spent many hours together trying to create Riff, from scar ideas to tattoos. Every single choice was specific. For example, there's the tattoo of a pinup girl on my right forearm, representing Queen Mab from the big Mercutio speech that he delivers to Romeo. Judy also handpicked a bunch of other tattoos and selected one that said "happy." I thought, *Oh man, Riff would absolutely wear a "happy" tattoo.* Lastly, during rehearsals, I just drew one, with lines coming down like a little jet plane. That became the Jet tattoo.

"Cool": Mike Faist (Riff) and Ansel Elgort (Tony)

"QUINTET"

Riff leads the Jets out of the chop shop and into the surrounding ruins.

Bernardo and the Sharks explode out the double doors of the warehouse which opens onto an alley and head towards the street.

Anita, Rosalía and Luz, veils on, kneeling in a pew among a sparse mostly female CONGREGATION . . .

Tony puts on his jacket and heads towards the ladder that leads to the alley behind the drugstore.

María is walking towards the subway in her working clothes. She seems to emerge out of the brilliant orange flare of the setting sun.

—from the script by Tony Kushner

DAVID NEWMAN (music arranger): The "Quintet" has five sections that by the end of the number are going on at the same time. We call it polyphony, meaning more than one melody going simultaneously. You have the Jets, the Sharks, Tony, María, and Anita. By the time you get to the end they're all doing counterpoint, much like in an opera.

MATTHEW SULLIVAN (executive music producer/music supervisor): Every single person who is in the movie makes an appearance in one way or another through the "Quintet." It's three and a half minutes of packed energy and a cacophony of vocals, following exactly what's happening with every character. Steven had a brilliant idea of getting these people from point A to point B and showing the story of what's to come, using it to amp up the energy of the movie. That's probably my favorite moment in the film.

TONY KUSHNER (screenwriter/ executive producer): The "Quintet" is amazing onstage, because you bring all the characters together in one magical place, created by the score, in which they retain their differences and yet make music together. Stage realism is less constraining than movie realism, because everything onstage is less real. So, it's easier to slip into something unreal onstage. Steven solved that, I think, by making the "Quintet" about two things film captures powerfully: velocity and light. He joined with the score's propulsive force to create a kind of vortex of movement, radiance, and darkness. The characters plunge through blinding light into the night, determined to act, carried forward from romance into tragedy.

JUSTIN PECK (choreographer): The "Quintet" is a beautiful assembly of many carefully planned-out shots of the two gangs, of Anita, of María, of Tony, all interweaving with each other and preparing for the rumble that evening. It's the turning point—the moment where everything's about to change.

Because it has a kind of montage effect, we shot this section in many pieces. Every once in a while, we'd shoot a five-second shot, which would be like one card in the deck that makes up the "Quintet." When Steven showed me his edit for the "Quintet," I was blown away by his vision in storytelling and assembly. It has so much momentum and adrenaline coursing through it.

MIKE FAIST (Riff): This is the one number in the show where you get to see everybody's point of view and how different they all are. On the one hand we have the Sharks, who are feeling threatened and ready to take on the Jets to prove once and for all that they deserve to be here. And the Jets share in the same spirit. Riff needs his boys and doesn't feel he actually can be the leader. He's having to step into this role and fake it. Then you have Tony, making a decision to try to stop the rumble in the name of love and dreaming that everything will be lovely and fine. It's a fascinating moment in the movie, because there's so much going on with each group, but they're singing the same thing.

JANUSZ KAMINSKI (director of photography): Our executive producer and first assistant director, Adam Somner, was amazing at creating a schedule that would allow for the story to be taken from one place to another through the course of the day and yet maintain the schedule. For example, certain musical numbers like the "Quintet" were filmed over several city blocks, and only certain small chunks would take place in one particular location. We constantly had to be moving the entire company, and the equipment. In terms of organization, you have to be prepared way in advance to accommodate the requirements of the filming. Sometimes you would shoot in a situation where the street would go into shadow where just five seconds prior, you were in full sunlight. The logistics alone were very complex on all levels and for everyone. There's no room for mistakes. You have to make sure that nobody gets injured, that everyone's safe. I spend my life making movies where everything is so well organized that it's hard to adjust back to the real world once we complete filming.

DAVID ALVAREZ (Bernardo): The "Quintet" had this quick rhythm—a battle rhythm—and you feel it through the movement, the acting, the singing. Jeanine Tesori was incredible at analyzing what the energy of the song was and making sure that the actors could apply that to it.

DAVID AVILÉS MORALES (Aníbal): Steven wanted to include our culture, and there are a lot of Puerto Rican flags in the movie. But in the fifties, the color of the flag was different. It was changed to look a little bit more like the American flag. The blue is a little bit darker than it was in the fifties. The production didn't know that—I mentioned it to them, and they changed every

flag on the movie. The day of the "Quintet," Steven handed me the flag, and I got to carry it during the scene. It was one of my proudest moments.

MIKE FAIST: There's a lovely Abraham Lincoln quote that goes, "Give me six hours to chop down a tree and I will spend the first four hours sharpening the ax." And that's the work that the Jets did. We really took the time to create and cultivate our relationships; when we were rolling camera, we were there. And that was it.

Shooting movies is the hardest thing in the world, because you're trying to focus and you have many other things going on around you. All I can remember really is just trying to stay as focused as possible and just be present. All I had to do was just turn around and look my Jets in the eyes. And off we went.

Weapons for "The Rumble," created by property master Diana Burton

"THE RUMBLE"

> Bernardo stops circling and walks towards Tony. The
> Sharks shout encouragement to Bernardo; the Jets shout
> encouragement to Tony, beneath which, exasperation. But
> Tony stands there, till Bernardo is close.
> —from the script by Tony Kushner

KRISTIE MACOSKO KRIEGER (producer): "The Rumble" marks the emotional climax of the film, so it was really important that we strike exactly the right tone. We shot the scene over six days of night shoots that ran from about 5:00 P.M. to 6:00 A.M. the next morning. While this filming schedule certainly created its own challenges, there were also a number of safety considerations due to a series of fight sequences and stunts. Mark Fichera, our stunt coordinator, was integral in choreographing the scene to ensure every member of the cast was safe and comfortable, while also making the scene realistic and believable. We had many rehearsals ahead of the shoot to get everything right, and I was so proud of how our cast brought this difficult and emotional scene to life.

STEVEN SPIELBERG (director/producer): For "The Rumble," we're using some of Robbins's moves—like when they open their arms to go on the attack, that is pure Robbins. But then it goes into Justin Peck's own interpretation of it after that. The fight itself is not a dance—it's real, it's realistic.

David Alvarez is one of those silent heroes; he never calls attention to himself, he's part of the company that's making the movie—until he steps in front of the camera as Bernardo, and then he becomes this beautiful boxer, moving and talking

like a natural-born king. He's earthshaking. All of our mouths fell open when we saw what David, Ansel, and Mike did at the bloody climax of "The Rumble." The loss of these three wonderful young guys—two of whom are dead and the third leaves needing to find a way to die—they made it heartrending.

ADAM STOCKHAUSEN (production designer): Instead of staging this scene underneath the West Side Highway, Tony Kushner suggested that "The Rumble" take place in a sanitation shed, where road salt is stored during the summer to be used in the winter. We were looking for this enormous space, and we actually found the site on the Brooklyn Navy Yard. The other critical requirement was that it had to have a lot of windows, because Steven wanted to feel the presence of the highway, and to have light strobing through as cars were passing by. We had real salt with a little tiny bit of cheating using some foam; it piled up really beautifully.

JUSTIN PECK (choreographer): It's important to share that there was no animosity between the Jets and the Sharks. On the contrary, they were quite supportive of each other and took inspiration from one another often. A beautiful camaraderie developed throughout the project, and the Jets and Sharks became a full band of brothers and sisters.

Top
Concept art by Stephen Tappin

Middle
A standoff between the Sharks and Jets

Bottom
Riff (Mike Faist) and Bernardo (David Alvarez) square up with their iconic switchblades in hand.

I think that they will be bonded for life, thanks to this experience.

GARY RYDSTROM (re-recording mixer/ sound designer): After having several near fights or metaphorical fights in the movie, we get to "The Rumble." This is a real fight. Our job is to make it threatening and dangerous.

The salt shed location is unique and a beautiful opportunity for something different. There are cars going by off-screen; you see the headlights go by through the windows, and we wanted to find sounds to make the ambience of the salt shed sound "cold."

As the cops arrive, you hear one of the key sounds for this movie: old-fashioned crank sirens. The most interesting part of those old sirens is that they don't just stop, they wind down. This is a good case of the real sound being the right sound emotionally for this moment.

MIKE FAIST (Riff): The entire movie is leading up toward "The Rumble," which is exactly what Riff wants; he thinks that if he can make a rumble happen with the Sharks, then Tony will have no choice but to come back as the leader of the Jets. But in our heads as actors, we were also gearing ourselves up toward it. It was one of those magical things where you find elements and pieces of yourself that you didn't know existed. One of those things, for me at least, was with David Alvarez at the moment where he stabbed me. We were looking into each other's eyes and there was this instant kind of

bond, a certain understanding of one another. It's this strange thing, looking into the eyes of someone that's taking your life.

DAVID ALVAREZ (Bernardo): I had to take boxing lessons for a couple of months before shooting. We also had a week of stunt training, where we started to learn how to fight for the camera. And then we did stunt training to learn how to fight with weapons, and finally we applied all of that to the choreography that we were going to use for the fight scenes and "The Rumble."

MIKE FAIST: Creating that knife fight with David and our stunt coordinator, Mark Fichera, was really something that the three of us crafted together—we wanted to show that both of these guys were scared for their lives, as opposed to just trying to kill the other person. We wanted to add in these elements of real fear.

MARK FICHERA (stunt coordinator): It could not be the same "dance fighting" that you see in the original film or on Broadway. This needed to show the real peril for the two gangs. They're out for blood. It's not this friendly game of back-and-forth. The audience has to feel that they're at odds with each other. The Sharks tend to hang out at a boxing gym. And so they're more technical when they fight. Bernardo has a little bit of a boxer's swagger. Whereas the Jets are more brawlers. They're street fighters

mainly, and they'll use weapons, dirty fighting.

We actually did a lot of research and looked at photos of street brawls, as well as footage of hooligan fights. It's not pretty. It's not choreographed. You're missing punches. You're slipping on the ground. We wanted to capture the frenetic energy of a real fight. We kept the choreography loose and focused on teaching the actors how to move for the screen. At the beginning, I was unsure of their level of experience. It was very clear that they are talented. They all just wanted to soak everything up. It was actually a blessing that they were all dancers and understood "safe spacing" and the elements of stunt work. They had to be taught the fundamentals. When you have raw talent and actors who are eager, the sky is the limit. For instance, with Mike Faist and Ansel, they were so diligent about infusing their character into the framework of the fights. It morphed over time, because as we rehearsed and they got more into character, they came back with ideas, and suggested a retreat instead of a lunge. It was fascinating to watch.

"The Rumble" was the biggest fight scene in the movie. We started training the actors for it during preproduction, because it was very clear you couldn't use stunt doubles. We had to get them all to the point where they could realistically fight on camera without hurting each other. We literally had a boot camp to train the actors and walk them through boxing,

Top
Riff (Mike Faist) attacks Bernardo (David Alvarez) with his switchblade.

Bottom
The death of Riff

reactions, falling, hitting the ground, how to sell things for camera. We used pre-viz [a rough animated version of the fight] to show them where the camera would be to make sure every punch would sell visually. And they learned along the way. "The Rumble" consists of three parts: In the beginning you have Bernardo and Tony fighting. And that's more of a boxing, hand-to-hand brawling fight. And then it escalates with a knife fight. It's obviously a life-and-death situation, and the tone changes dramatically. That shift was very important to Steven. The final stage involves the group after Riff has been stabbed, and they go into a big brawl. It's an all-out war at that point, and it's "dirty fighting." Everybody's trying to get retaliation. Everyone's out for blood.

DIANA BURTON (property master): All the weapons at "The Rumble" were found objects. We copied the real weapons, made casts of them, and made versions with different kinds of rubber: a soft rubber and a harder rubber, depending on how they were being used at a given moment. Whenever possible, we gave the actors the real weapons.

As written in the script, Riff, being the leader, has a baseball bat, which he uses like a scepter. When I was looking for the two switchblades, one couldn't be longer than the other. Bernardo's has a bone handle, which was quite exquisite and beautiful, and Riff's has a strictly black handle.

Top
Bernardo (David Alvarez) stands back after delivering the killing blow.

Bottom
Tony (Ansel Elgort) rushes to his fallen friend and takes up his knife.

ANSEL ELGORT (Tony): "The Rumble" was intense and shot at night. It was physical and emotional. We always had to be out of breath, so everyone was doing jumping jacks, pull-ups, push-ups, running, and trying to be as physically present as possible.

JESS LePROTTO (A-Rab): It was not so much about the emotion; it was about how do I maintain the emotion and how do I keep it consistent from take to take. The laser-sharp focus required to interpret this material was the key. We as a unit knew how extremely important it was to hold on to that energy. And I know that all of us were very proud to go through what we did to get to that point as a group.

DAVID ALVAREZ: "The Rumble" brought back memories of being in the army. We were tired, we were hungry, we were getting angry, we were fighting in the scenes, and it got pretty intense. Everyone was emotional, but there was also this huge sense of camaraderie.

This is my first movie, and it is completely different from doing a show on Broadway. For me, once you step on a stage, you're sucked into that world until you step out of it. You have to be involved in the character you play for two hours, nonstop, and that takes a toll on you every night. With film, you show up, you think about your scene, and then once they say "action" you snap into your character, you do the scene. Once they say "cut" you snap out of it. Or you can try some method acting and stay

in character as well. I tried to find a balance, especially during "The Rumble." I found it was easier for me to stay connected to Bernardo that entire week we filmed the scene.

DAVID AVILÉS MORALES (Aníbal): During "The Rumble," it was really surprising the way that we embraced our characters and how we could switch the hate that we're supposed to feel in the film to the love that we felt for one another outside the story.

EZRA MENAS (Anybodys): You could feel the tension. Usually we liked to have fun, but when we were in the salt shed, as soon as you stepped in front of the camera, everyone was very focused. We knew the emotional weight of what we were dealing with, and how relevant it still is.

ANDREI CHAGAS (Jochi): At "The Rumble," I became so angry. At that moment, you understand how you can lose yourself completely, you don't know what's happening, you don't know what's around you because your sense of judgment is just completely lost.

ANSEL ELGORT: From time to time Steven will ask the person who's usually off camera to do something specific for the benefit of the actor who is having their shot. For instance, during "The Rumble," he asked Mike to tell me that he loved me as I looked up at him, after beating Bernardo almost to death. . . . With those few words from Mike, I had something new to react to.

DAVID ALVAREZ: Bernardo never means to kill Riff; it happens by accident. But once that happens, there's no turning back. Once Riff is killed, that starts a vicious cycle of violence that is only stopped once María steps in, at the end of the movie.

PATRICK HIGGINS (Baby John): We all know *West Side Story*. We all know how it goes, but seeing Mike Faist get stabbed just over and over and over again, seeing the tears in his eyes and just the helplessness of it all, had everybody crying; I didn't expect that to happen at all. It was really a somber experience.

ANSEL ELGORT: On one of the days during "The Rumble," when Riff was dying in front of me, for some reason I wasn't getting that emotional reaction. We were on take five at that point, and Riff getting stabbed with a knife probably should have warranted a more explosive emotional reaction from me. In the previous coverage we did from the side, I did have that reaction. We moved to my coverage, with the camera right in my face, and I wasn't in it. Steven comes over, and this is the nicest way a director could ever pull this out of you. He looked at me and said, "You're not bringing it. You're not bringing it." Just remembering it is getting me emotional; it made me feel so terrible but in the nicest way. We did the next take, and we got it.

DAVID ALVAREZ: During my death scene, Steven just whispered in my ear, "Remember the kid you were." I just kept playing what he said in my head, and the emotions came flooding in.

BEN COOK (Mouthpiece): Everyone just gave each other the space and time to be and live in that world. People cried; people sobbed even. But coming out on the other side of that week, I think we were all bonded on a whole other level.

KYLE COFFMAN (Ice): I don't know if I'll ever experience anything like that again. But that's why you become an artist; it's to hopefully experience moments like that. I have such gratitude for the care, the commitment, and the beauty of the storytelling that we were all a part of.

MIKE FAIST: With Steven, what I witnessed and saw was a person who is just chasing his joy. He would show up with an openness that would allow everyone to learn along the way. In my opinion, he is the perfect artist, because he remains a student. He remains curious. When he's not shooting, he tells me he's studying footage. He's watching the shots. Here's a guy who just loves what he does and chooses to do that in its simplest form. That really was infectious for everyone.

Following spread, top right
Ansel Elgort (Tony) and David Alvarez (Bernardo)

Following spread, center right
Julius Anthony Rubio (Quique), assistant director Adam Somner, David Alvarez, Ansel Elgort, and Mike Faist (Riff) filming "The Rumble"

Following spread, bottom right
Producer Kristie Macosko Krieger and Steven Spielberg

Opposite
Storyboards by Raymond Prado

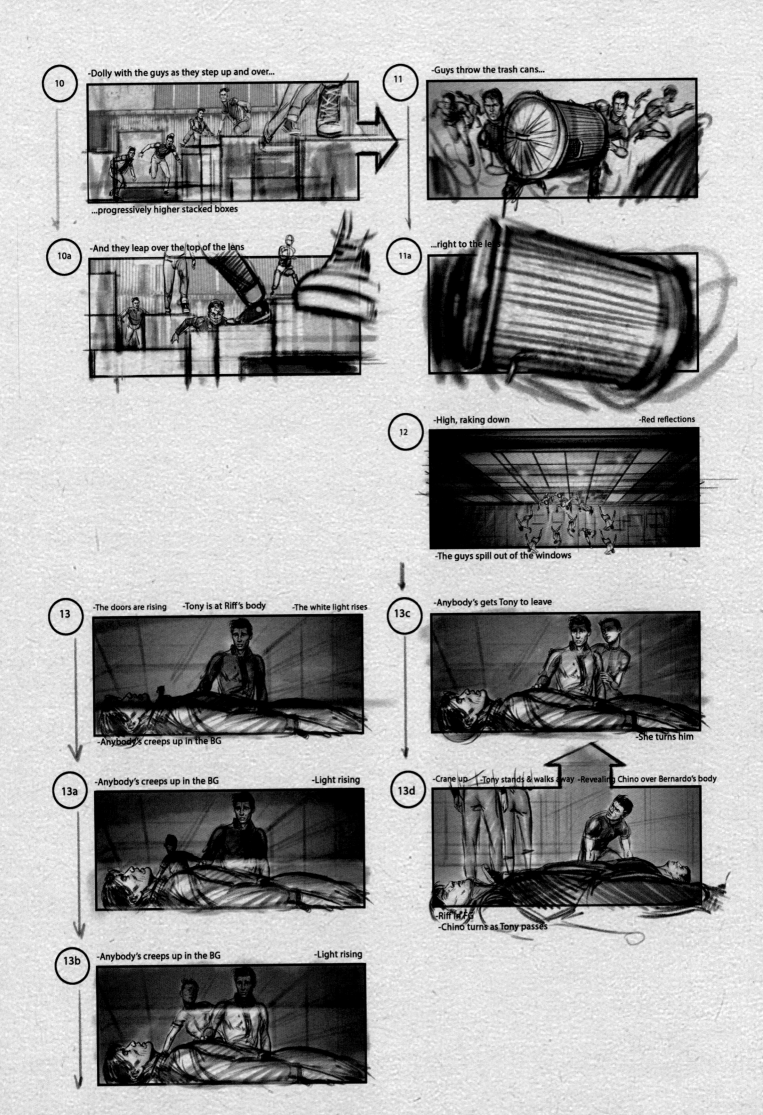

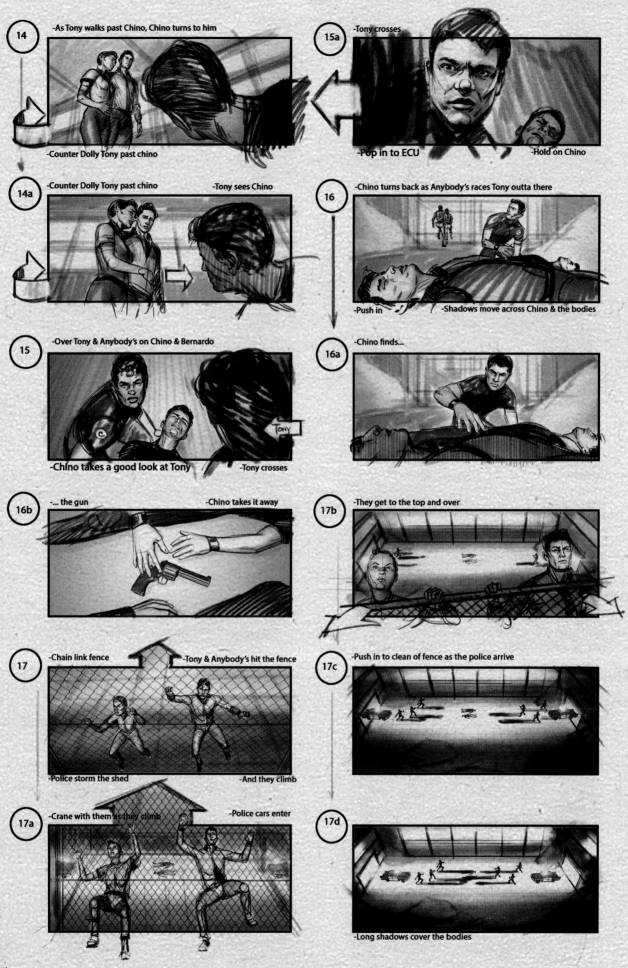

14 -As Tony walks past Chino, Chino turns to him
-Counter Dolly Tony past chino

15a -Tony crosses
-Pop in to ECU
-Hold on Chino

14a -Counter Dolly Tony past chino
-Tony sees Chino

16 -Chino turns back as Anybody's races Tony outta there
-Push in
-Shadows move across Chino & the bodies

15 -Over Tony & Anybody's on Chino & Bernardo
-Chino takes a good look at Tony
-Tony crosses

16a -Chino finds...

16b -... the gun
-Chino takes it away

17b -They get to the top and over

17 -Chain link fence
-Tony & Anybody's hit the fence
-Police storm the shed
-And they climb

17c -Push in to clean of fence as the police arrive

17a -Crane with them as they climb
-Police cars enter

17d -Long shadows cover the bodies

This page
Storyboards by Raymond Prado

Opposite
Lining up the climactic end to "The Rumble." From left: 2nd A camera operator Connie Huang, makeup department head Judy Chin, Garett Hawe (Skink), Patrick Higgins (Baby John).
Foreground: Ansel Elgort (Tony) and David Alvarez (Bernardo)

"I FEEL PRETTY"

> María (. . .), dusting a display of gringa
> mannequins in cocktail dresses, martini glasses in
> a fancy modern apartment, on the wall above: WITTY
> WEAR WITH BRIGHT AUTUMN FLAIR! María's examining a
> mannequin's brocade stole.
>   —from the script by Tony Kushner

DAVID NEWMAN (music arranger): With "I Feel Pretty," one can make it sound like a military waltz, kind of heavy, not childlike, but with Gustavo Dudamel conducting, it becomes lighter; they're girls dancing, having fun and playfully mocking María. He kept saying, "This is not a military piece. It's teenage girls dressing up." He got a wonderful sound and texture out of the New York and Los Angeles Philharmonics.

TONY KUSHNER (screenwriter/producer): In the original stage version, "I Feel Pretty" was the opening song at the top of Act Two, after the intermission that follows the rumble that ends Act One. In other words, when María sang "I Feel Pretty," the audience knew that María's life is over, that the man she loves has murdered her brother. It's a shocking thing to do, dramaturgically—so shocking that when I started work on the screenplay by listening to the original Broadway cast album over and over, it took me several listens to take in what they'd done. I cried when it finally sank in. It's a brilliant, heartbreaking, risky choice. "I Feel Pretty" is like "I Could Have Danced All Night" in *My Fair Lady*, it's a moment of sheer musical ecstasy. But in the original production, Robbins, and Bernstein and Sondheim and Laurents, were resolute in trying to make a musical tragedy, which

María (Rachel Zegler) reflects in front of one of Gimbels's many mirrors.

meant casting the shadows of death and loss over hope and joy. I called Steven and said, "You have to promise me that we're going to keep this song after 'The Rumble,' where it belongs." And we did.

Sondheim doesn't like his lyrics for "I Feel Pretty." He's often disparaged the line "I feel pretty and witty and bright," saying that it sounds more like Noël Coward than a Puerto Rican teenager in 1957. I wondered where a Puerto Rican teenager might have picked up this frothy Anglo palaver and why she'd want to make lighthearted use of it. I'd been considering changing María's place of employment from a bridal shop to something less romantic and more reflective of the kind of employment opportunities available to her—for instance, a late-night cleaning crew at a large department store, in which she would be surrounded by displays and placards promoting the style of the era: chic, sophisticated, pretty and witty and bright. María resents the witty, pretty people she has to clean up after, but she also envies their relative wealth and comfort, and like all of us, she's susceptible to conventions of glamour and romance. I think the song works beautifully as something simultaneously parodic and playfully participatory. And the cleaning crew gave us a way to increase the number of women singing the song, from three to eight, which makes it bigger and more joyful and inclusive.

Opposite, top
Concept art by Stephen Tappin

Opposite, center and bottom; this page
Rachel Zegler (María) and Steven Spielberg on the Gimbels set with Annelise Cepero (Provi), Jamila Velazquez (Meche), Ilda Mason (Luz), and Ana Isabelle (Rosalía)

RACHEL ZEGLER (María): I love the way "I Feel Pretty" begins as a self-realization that she feels beautiful. She just goes and has fun with the number. And in a way, "I Feel Pretty" is almost a dance or natural movement of a woman in love. Justin Peck and I worked a lot together on how María would react to the environment in that scene. There's a cut of "I Feel Pretty" that Steven made early on, on his iPhone, using the rehearsal footage that ended up being completely different from what we eventually shot on set in Newark, New Jersey. Steven always had a vision, but it was really awesome to see it change and evolve for that particular scene. He would ask, "What do you think María does in this scene? What do you think her reaction is?" And we would have a conversation about it. He is not the type of director who tells you what to do and you have to do it. It's a conversation. And he does that every day on set with everybody.

ADAM STOCKHAUSEN (production designer): It's really exciting to have María working at the department store. It expands the scope of the world; it is very useful for the social hierarchy of the story. There's the wonderful line that says, "You don't shop at Gimbels, you clean at Gimbels," and that's really an important statement. My mother actually worked at Gimbels, so I was always aware of

it, and it was exciting to be able to re-create it. We found a space in New Jersey, at an old bank building with a grand old atrium lobby area, and then created a mid-century set inside of it. The song "I Feel Pretty" was all about reflection; therefore, María is seeing herself in mirrors through the course of the song, from small dressing mirrors at cosmetics counters to the big trifold dressing mirrors. Steven was able to build shots with endless reflections.

GARY RYDSTROM (re-recording mixer/ sound designer): The setup of the scene provides an opportunity to showcase the underlying tragedy that's just happened, and we start the scene with rain and thunder, giving a sense that there's something bad out there that the characters don't know about yet.

"SOMEWHERE"

```
INT. DOC'S DRUGSTORE - LATE NIGHT

    On the wall behind the counter, there are photos of

Valentina as a bride with Doc; the couple together;

Doc as an old man. Valentina takes down a photo of

Doc. Looking at it, she sits at the counter, and pours

herself a drink. She blows the photo a kiss, then

drinks, then looks towards the door.

    ("Somewhere" begins . . .)

    —from the script by Tony Kushner
```

TONY KUSHNER (screenwriter/executive producer): I asked Steven if we could give "Somewhere" to Valentina. It wasn't sung by Tony and María in the stage musical, and I loved the idea of hearing Rita Moreno sing it. I felt it'd make a powerful connection between the era the musical depicts and the present day, hearing this song of hope and yearning for a better world sung by a woman who's been a witness to, and important participant in, the tormented world we inhabit. It makes us think about where we were as a society when we first heard the song, and where we are now. When she sang it at our big table reading, there wasn't a dry eye in the room.

DAVID NEWMAN (music arranger): The idea of it is to sound raw and devastating. It's almost a capella, with a held string note and a piano.

RITA MORENO (Valentina): "Somewhere" was used as a ballet in the original Broadway production. You didn't see the singer. Barbra Streisand recorded a beautiful rendition of it. When I came on this new film, I knew I wasn't going to dance. But then I saw that Tony had Valentina singing "Somewhere," and I couldn't believe it. It's such an extraordinary song of belief and hope. What an experience that was. I hope the audience is as moved by it as I was performing it.

Kushner's script infuses new meaning into the song by giving it to the character of Valentina. But Rita's performance of "Somewhere" felt like a full-circle moment. Seeing her bring her talent and legacy to our film and watching her pass the baton off to the next generation of young Latinx performers was deeply moving.

KRISTIE MACOSKO KRIEGER (producer): Watching Rita sing "Somewhere" was truly a special moment. We closed the set to create an intimate environment, and Rita just knocked it out of the park. Tony

JANUSZ KAMINSKI (director of photography): Having Rita in the movie made it even more special, because she represents the continuation of the legacy of *West Side Story*. She would talk about what it was like to make the first movie, the good things and the tough things about it. She helped with the authenticity of the dialogue and the behavioral aspect of the actors who played the Puerto Rican parts. She was the maternal figure of this movie.

Opposite
Rita Moreno (Valentina) and Ansel Elgort (Tony)

Above
Screenwriter/executive producer Tony Kushner (left) shares a moment with Steven Spielberg and Rita Moreno.

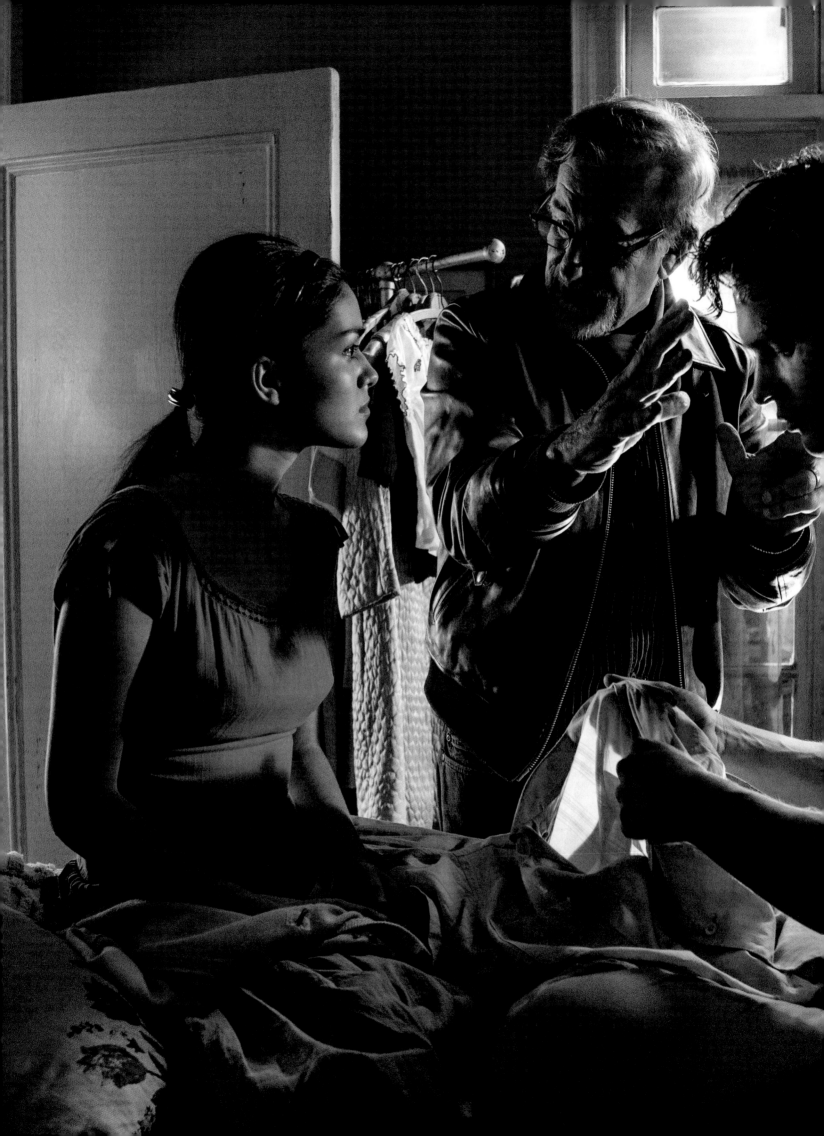

"A BOY LIKE THAT / I HAVE A LOVE"

```
Anita slaps María, hard.
("A Boy Like That / I Have a Love" begins:)
They stand, shocked by the slap. Anita leaves the
bedroom. María follows her.
        —from the script by Tony Kushner
```

STEVEN SPIELBERG (director/producer): "A Boy Like That" is a pursuit. Anita aggressively pursues María through the rooms of the apartment they share. "A boy like that" refers to Tony, who killed her brother. . . . "Forget that boy and find another." María finally defends herself and her love for Tony. She turns around and she starts pursuing Anita into a retreat. The scene is choreographed; it's not a dance, but it has movement. I storyboarded all of this months before we ever got to the set.

TONY KUSHNER (screenwriter/executive producer): "A Boy Like That/I Have a Love" comes to *West Side Story* from the realm of grand opera. It's vocal cord busting and dramatically demonic. María has to stay in love with a guy who murdered her brother. Anita has to forgive María for loving Tony. That's a tall order, making us believe love can surmount even obstacles like that. Our two remarkable actresses, under Steven's direction, singing Sondheim's words and Bernstein's music, make you believe in the all-conquering power of love.

ARIANA DeBOSE (Anita): I love that Steven was not afraid to dive into the grief of it all. There's an intense feeling, in particular with Anita. You get to observe her in those moments of coming home to her apartment knowing that the love of her life

Steven Spielberg and his two leads

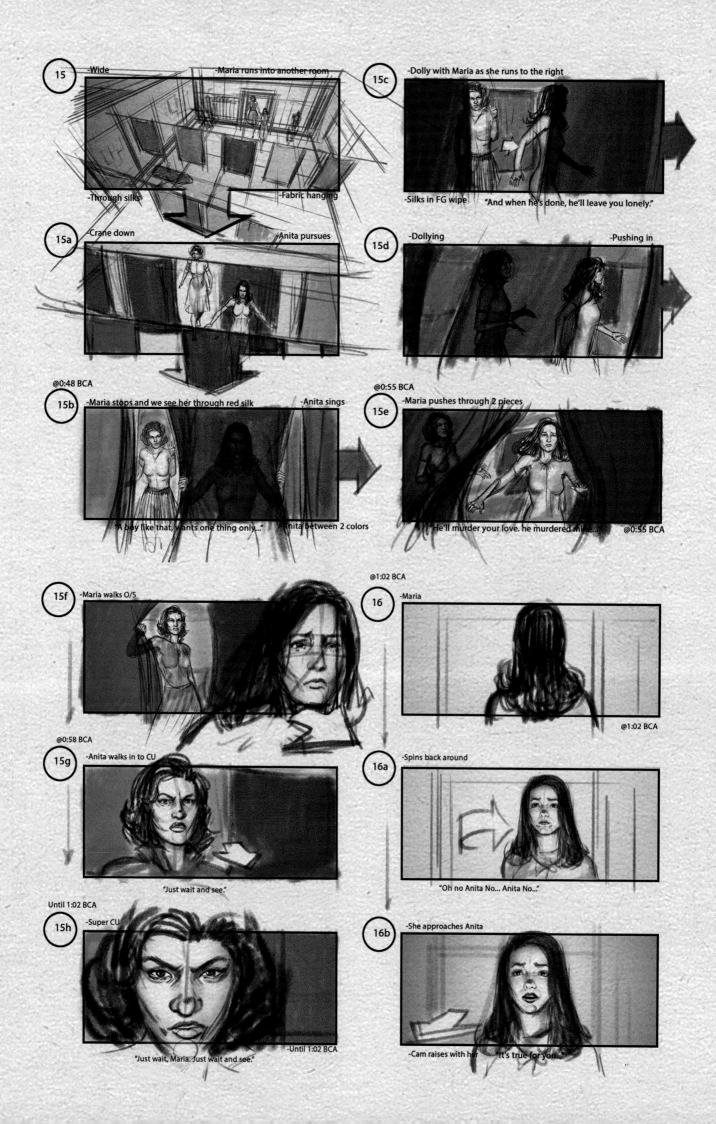

15 -Wide — -Maria runs into another room
-Through silks — -Fabric hanging

15a -Crane down — Anita pursues

15b @0:48 BCA
-Maria stops and we see her through red silk — -Anita sings
"A boy like that, wants one thing only…" — -Anita between 2 colors

15f -Maria walks O/S

15g @0:58 BCA
-Anita walks in to CU
"Just wait and see."

15h Until 1:02 BCA
-Super CU
"Just wait, Maria. Just wait and see." — -Until 1:02 BCA

15c -Dolly with Maria as she runs to the right
-Silks in FG wipe — "And when he's done, he'll leave you lonely."

15d -Dollying — -Pushing in

15e @0:55 BCA
-Maria pushes through 2 pieces
"He'll murder your love. he murdered mine…" — @0:55 BCA

@1:02 BCA
16 -Maria
@1:02 BCA

16a -Spins back around
"Oh no Anita No… Anita No…"

16b -She approaches Anita
-Cam raises with her — "It's true for you…"

is gone—and that she has to tell María the truth, because presumably she doesn't realize that María already knows. You witnessed her having to identify a body. You're going on that journey with her, and it's terrifying. I remember first reading it being totally shaken; there're some moments in life you run to, and others where you walk as slowly as possible in apprehension of confronting reality. You get the sense of deep despair, of horror, fear. You also get to see people slight her in her moment of grief. You watch police officers treat her like she is not deserving of compassion. Going through that journey with her eventually gets us to "I Have a Love," where she realizes and acknowledges that while her time of love has passed, María has an opportunity to continue with Tony, and, ultimately, Anita finds the strength to support María.

TONY KUSHNER: It feels breathtakingly cruel when María sings to Anita,

"You were in love—or so you said,

You should know better . . ."

Anita's just lost Bernardo, the love of her life, and María seems to tell this grieving woman that her love is a sham, a pretense. But the severity of this blow is what forces Anita out of the despair engulfing her; it forces her to return to the world of the living, to the very young woman who needs her help. Ariana, Rachel, and Steven illuminated this for me. The song changes from the bitterest of fights to a scene between a mother and daughter. It's unbearably sad, but it's a stunning moment.

Opposite
Storyboards by Raymond Prado

This page
Ariana DeBose (Anita) and Rachel Zegler (María)

VIOLENCE AT DOC'S

> Numbers starts to dance around Anita, an obscene
> parody of the mambo.
>
> (. . .)
>
> Balkan joins in with Numbers, dancing around Anita,
> rubbing against her, pulling at her clothes. Anita
> shoves Numbers away, hard. This gets the other Jets
> excited. One by one, they start to join the dance.
>
> —from the script by Tony Kushner

PATRICK HIGGINS (Baby John): After Riff has been killed, the Jets are at Doc's drugstore, just mourning him, not really saying much, not really talking to each other. They just seem very quiet. My audition for Baby John was that scene. It's a strong moment for my character, as he gets to the anger and finally bursts out. He is the only one who is saying, "This is real, you guys don't understand. This is real life. He's gone. We're never going to get him back, and you guys don't get it." And it just goes right back to complete silence. It's really powerful.

MARK FICHERA (stunt coordinator): The Jets harass Anita, dance around her, and then it escalates into violence. It's one of those situations where you have a marriage of dance choreography with the genius of Justin Peck, and stunts.

KRISTIE MACOSKO KRIEGER (producer): We knew we needed to approach that scene with care and respect for our actors. The production team brought in an intimacy coordinator/advisor to work with the Jets on the mechanics of that moment, and to ensure Ariana felt safe and comfortable both in rehearsals and through filming. We were also lucky to have Patricia Delgado, who brought

An intense moment at Doc's with Rita Moreno (Valentina), Ariana DeBose (Anita), and the Jets (Sean Harrison Jones as Action, second from left, and Garett Hawe as Skink)

her own perspective as a female dancer to the blocking and choreography of that scene.

ARIANA DeBOSE (Anita): The scene of the attempted rape of Anita comes hot off the heels of the deaths of Riff and Bernardo. Anita goes to the drugstore in search of Tony to give him a message from María. That's where the Jets have chosen to congregate after the tragedy of the rumble. There is a moment where you can feel Anita realizing that if she goes into the store, she will not leave as she came in. And she does not. I did my fair share of listening to personal and heartbreaking accounts. While filming it, there were moments where I did feel overwhelmed, but I was lucky that the group of young men involved in that scene have a deep affection for me, and I for them. While they were truly acting, there was still love there that I could feel that made it okay. It is very hard to tell a story like that and not lose yourself. We played the truth, and it's there for everyone to see, hopefully be moved by it, and realize this is unacceptable. It's something that just happens in the spur of a moment of intense grief. But it does not excuse the behavior.

KEVIN CSOLAK (Diesel): We all had to dive into this dark mindset and go where we didn't want to go. We had Ariana, who is a dream to work with, and we were all briefed by an intimacy coach beforehand. Even with

that, after every take, we had to sit there for a second, and just breathe and shake it off.

TALIA RYDER (Tessa): The scene at Doc's—given the nature of the scene—was a completely different experience from "Dance at the Gym." Since the scene involved such sensitive subject matter, the process was much more intimate. Even though I was only sixteen at the time, Steven treated me and the other minors like adults and didn't shield us from the darkness of the scene. The set was more of a solemn place than it was shooting "Dance at the Gym" but still was filled with the same amount of love and curiosity.

PALOMA GARCIA-LEE (Graziella): The women in this version of *West Side Story* are not two-dimensional. These are three-dimensional women who are very strong, have points of view, and are very inspiring. There is a rivalry, there is tension, and then there's love and support. You see it in the drugstore scene, where Graziella tries to save Anita when she is being assaulted by the Jets, until Valentina comes in and goes to bat for Anita. It's this moment where women are banding together to stand up and support each other despite our differences. That's a very important message we're telling, then and now. Steven approached the scene with great care, awareness, and at the end of each day, we would all hug each other and breathe together. It ended up being very connective for us as actors.

Top
Ariana DeBose (Anita)

Bottom
From left: Patrick Higgins (Baby John), Kevin Csolak (Diesel), Ariana DeBose, and Kyle Coffman (Ice)

"FINALE"

The first bullet from Chino's gun hits Tony from
behind, in his shoulder. It knocks him forward, but he
doesn't fall; he stumbles a few steps towards María,
then stops, confused. María is looking past him.

Behind Tony, at the other end of the street, Chino
aims his gun.

—from the script by Tony Kushner

RACHEL ZEGLER (María): We did the sad and final scene on the streets of Paterson, New Jersey, and there was a weird weight in the air. . . . It was the dead of night, as it would be in real time. Everything was quiet except for police sirens, and that's exactly what happens in that last scene. . . . Everything is quiet and then the police car arrives.

TONY KUSHNER (screenwriter/executive producer): Because Valentina [Rita Moreno] sings "Somewhere," I worried I'd created a problem. At the end of the musical, María reprises "Somewhere" as Tony dies in her arms. But we'd made it Valentina's song, so it makes no sense for María to reprise something she's never heard and doesn't know. "Somewhere" is a great, great song, but I thought about what it says, and I began to feel that maybe it wasn't as perfect a song for her to sing to Tony in extremis. She's promising him that they'll be reunited in some wonderful place, which is sweet, but . . . is it true? Maybe, but wouldn't she want to promise him something they can both be certain of? Wouldn't she feel he needs this certainty? That made me think about what Tony sings to her at the beginning of "Tonight":

"Only you, you're the only thing I'll see forever
In my eyes, in my words, and in everything I do
Nothing else but you, ever."

One last moment together: María (Rachel Zegler) and Tony (Ansel Elgort)

In this dreadful moment, this is the one thing María knows about the future, the one thing she can give him: "I'll never let you go. I'll never forget you. You're going to be with me, in me forever."

ANSEL ELGORT (Tony): When we were doing my death scene, Steven asked me to speak to Rachel. He said, "Just talk to her. Tell her you love her." I whispered in her ear those words until she felt something. Steven is amazing that way. He knows how to pull great performances out of people.

RACHEL ZEGLER: I remember specifically Steven telling Ansel to talk to me during the death scene. I was crying while Ansel was just whispering beautiful things in my ear about how Tony is going be fine.

After Tony is dead, we did the scene where María is pointing the gun at Chino. Steven said to me, "I want you to hear in your mind Tony telling you that this isn't the way." That definitely spoke to me. But beyond that final moment, I kept asking myself, *How does María move on? How does she get over it?*

JANUSZ KAMINSKI (director of photography): Steven and I encourage each other. That's the beauty of the relationship, and we are supportive of choices that are not ordinary. We constantly think of the movie. But case in point, one day, we finished shooting, and as I'm driving toward Manhattan, I see this beautiful, soft, delicate light with buildings reflected in the water, and I'm thinking, *My God, it would be just so amazing to have that end the movie.* I get home, and Steven calls with the exact same idea. So, as they're carrying Tony's body at the end, the light just starts breaking through.

GARY RYDSTROM (re-recording mixer/ sound designer): This final scene of the movie, in which there's violence in front of Doc's, is very different ambience-wise from the rest of the movie. New York has always been alive with sounds. Even at night, there's always a sense of activity and people; it's a city that never sleeps. This scene was shot and designed to look very empty. Dead, with steam billowing in the background, and there's a look to it that's

a little more stylized. The sound does the same thing with billowing steam and some howling that's there almost subliminally. There's a sadness to the ambience, and that's a good setting for what's going to happen.

When Chino shoots Tony, we used elements from the original movie, with it reverberating off the buildings on the street.

KYLE COFFMAN (Ice): In the scene after Tony has been killed, the Sharks and the Jets are looking at each other. The Jets start to carry Tony's body, his arm falls down, and one of the Sharks comes in to help. Other Sharks join in. Suddenly, we all lift him together. The final shot reveals Sharks and Jets working together through the tragedy that brought them together. It took something that extreme to make them see the light. The last message is them exiting together as one. Filming that moment was a very interesting mix of having to be extremely technical and being on the right marks and the right angles for the different cameras and the need to project a very emotional storytelling moment.

ARIANA DeBOSE (Anita): There's a lot of darkness and a lot of hate, but the hope is that they do carry on, that they do it in a way that transcends bitterness. *West Side Story* is a story about love. Unconditional love. It's about people in the margins who are just trying to find their place in the world and hold on to love where they can find it, in whatever way. It could be Tony and Valentina with a motherly love he was never allowed to have. Brotherly love between Riff and Tony, Bernardo and Chino. Sisterly love between María and Anita. Brotherly love among the Sharks, and among the Jets. It's all about love and how it can carry you through. It can destroy you, but it can be your saving grace.

Opposite
In one of the film's most powerful scenes, Steven Spielberg works with Josh Andrés Rivera (Chino) to draw out a heartbreaking performance.

This page
Jets and Sharks unify after Tony's tragic death.

EXIT

STEVEN SPIELBERG (director/producer): The message of *West Side Story* is what is going to live forever. It is even more timely today than it was in 1957, when they mounted the production on Broadway. Even more timely than it was with the film in '61–'62. What it's about is what we are living in this country today—a time of tragic division and distrust, and the waste of human life through violence, racism, and xenophobia. And even though the story is a tragedy, like all great tragedies, including *Romeo And Juliet*, *West Side Story* suggests that hope can be born amid devastation and despair, and thanks to Bernstein and Sondheim's score, there's a feeling that despite all the sorrow and ugliness, love transcends. So don't ever give up! That's why I wanted to tell this story right now. It is even more about now than it was about then.

There are so many people who worked on the film I want to thank. We were a company. We were an ensemble. And we couldn't have done any of this without any of us doing the best work we've ever done, from the beginners to the veterans.

I am also so grateful to the person who sat next to me and read the script page by page: my wife, Kate. We listened to the music and we were bawling our eyes out; by the end of that, Kate turned to me and said, "You're going to make this movie. There is no arguing about it. It's just a matter of what you need to do to get ready for this." Kate was the one who lit the fire under me, and my producer, Kristie Macosko Krieger, was the one who set my clothes on fire. She said, "When do you want to start rolling?" And when I replied it would be nice if we could do it in June [2019], Kristie, Daniel Lupi [executive producer/unit production manager], and Adam Somner [executive producer/first assistant director] got together and made it happen.

Jets, Sharks, choreographers, and Steven Spielberg come together after filming "The Rumble."

RITA MORENO (Valentina): I did the final clap for the last take of the original [1961] *West Side Story*, and [director] Robert Wise said that was my wrap gift. So I asked Steven if I could do that [on this new production], and he agreed.

Working with Steven Spielberg has been probably the best experience of my life. He's really an actor's director. He thinks things through, he sees the logic of a scene, and he's a very cerebral person, which for some reason, I didn't expect. He is so cinematic. I will always be grateful to him for giving me this role.

VIRGINIA SÁNCHEZ KORROL (historical consultant): It's very important that all of our communities have their stories told, respected, and told from their point of view. That's what makes a strong nation. Ours is a nation of immigrants. American society is made up of multitudes of different people. The narrative of this country has to be one that is inclusive, not selective. It isn't just the story of one group of people. It isn't just the story of one set of founding fathers. It's a story that goes way beyond that. That narrative has to be told in media, films, and television programs.

Steven Spielberg is so aware of righting wrongs, of telling the stories that are not always told, of making films that make a difference. Through his work he adds to what we can learn about ourselves in ways that just can't be done in other areas. He delivers a message of openness, acceptance, and eagerness to learn.

ALEXANDER BERNSTEIN (son of Leonard Bernstein): Anybody of any age coming to see this movie will absolutely find something to relate to, be moved and inspired by it.

JAMIE BERNSTEIN (daughter of Leonard Bernstein): I don't think my father would be surprised that *West Side Story* is still going strong; everyone had already decided in his lifetime that this was a classic, a gem of musical theater, and that it would stick around. But I do think he would be a little surprised, and maybe disappointed, that the urgency of the story is still so powerful. He would have hoped that by now things would be getting better in our country when it comes to immigration and racism. He'd be pretty heartbroken to see our state of affairs today.

JUSTIN PECK (choreographer): The film represents almost a year of my life. I've learned so much. I've built some really incredible relationships that I know I will carry on into the future. Patricia [Delgado] and I call this project our honeymoon, because we got married in January and started working together on this almost right away. I started my journey into dance after seeing the original *West Side Story* film as a young kid. It led me to think: Maybe I can dance like that, too. All that said, *West Side Story* has now brought me full circle in the most unexpected way. It has been the honor of a lifetime. And ultimately, I hope that this new film will do for young people what the original film did for me: inspire the next generation of dancers.

RACHEL ZEGLER (María): This film is very poignant—that's the best word for it. The idea that "there's a place for us" from the song "Somewhere" is very important right now. People need to see what happens when hatred is fueled. This story is a perfect illustration of that. People die when hate is rampant. People think that their words don't really mean anything, but the second someone in power talks against a group for their skin color, their culture, their nationality, the whole world starts to speak that way. This movie is also correcting the way the original movie was made with the proper casting. There's no dubbing of vocals. The accents are accurate. We are not airbrushed to look darker than we are. And there's probably no one else who loves and understands *West Side Story* more than Steven Spielberg.

JANUSZ KAMINSKI (director of photography): It was a very challenging film to make, but it was also stimulating and artistically rewarding. It was like a strong workout: Your bones are hurting, but you feel a tremendous sense of accomplishment. The hot weather made it difficult to get through the day, but I couldn't wait to go back to set. Watching Steven being invigorated by the process was great. It's a process that doesn't exist anymore in the movies, and to be part of such a legacy was pretty amazing.

Steven Spielberg wraps the Sharks.

MICHAEL KAHN (editor): We had a first cut done by the time Steven finished filming; he selects his favorite takes as he goes, and we pretty much saw the finished film immediately. And then we kept running it over and over, making small changes. Steven spent a lot of time in the cutting room, and I have to say, none of us ever got bored with watching the film. Going into it, I thought it would be a lot more challenging to edit a musical—but it all came naturally. One of my favorite scenes in the film is a small dialogue scene in the kitchen, between Bernardo and María; they have an argument about the Jets and the gang warfare going on. You can really appreciate the amazing performances, and it feels very intimate. I really enjoyed editing that scene.

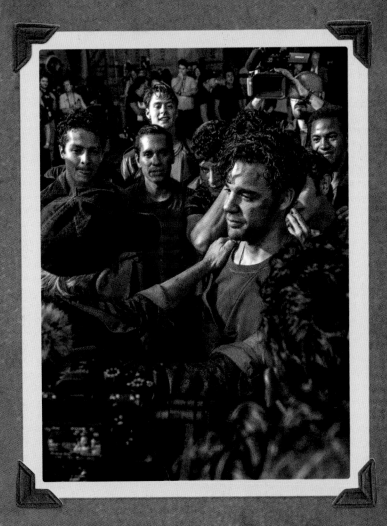

SARAH BROSHAR (editor): One luxury we had on this film was time. We've had a chance to go over and over the dailies, look for new things, take a step back, watch the film again, make small changes. It's been a treat to keep exploring and refining the film, and part of why we've kept watching and cutting is because we've enjoyed this project so much. The one thing I learned, or relearned, is that the simplest cut or edit of a scene is always the best way to go, especially with drama.

JOHN WILLIAMS (music consultant): Steven Spielberg is, unquestionably, one of our greatest filmmakers, and we can all look forward to Steven bringing his own vision of this masterpiece to the screen.

KRISTIE MACOSKO KRIEGER (producer): Hope, love, and community are everywhere in *West Side Story*, as in life. Despite tragedy, over and over humans continue to break down walls of prejudice and division through love. It is devastating that the racism and hate as depicted in this story are still so relatable sixty years after this show first came to Broadway. But it is important to note that the film ends with musical echoes from "Somewhere," and a message of hope. Working with Steven Spielberg is always a joy, but watching him challenge himself by tackling a new genre and championing this incredible cast of young, talented performers was one of the most energizing experiences of my entire career. It was truly a privilege to work with people at the top of their craft day in and day out, everyone from our dedicated crew members to our top-notch creative team to our extraordinarily talented cast and background actors. I'll never forget this experience, how much it humbled me, and how it reminded me why I love what I do.

TONY KUSHNER (screenwriter/ executive producer): For this project, I listened to each song dozens of times. I never got tired of any of them; it's inexhaustibly beautiful. Working on this material was a great gift. We didn't make this with the aim of replacing the spectacular 1961 film. My hope for it is that people will feel how much we love this musical, that we've served it well, and that we've given the world a new version of *West Side Story*.

STEVEN SPIELBERG: This is one production I never wanted to see end. I have had the greatest time making *West Side Story*. The last time I had a great time making a movie to this level was *E.T.* in 1981, and that movie certainly put in my head fatherhood and all sorts of things I never contemplated. Maybe this movie put in my head musicals and things I always have contemplated but until this time had never really had the courage to do.

Rita Moreno (Valentina) does the last clapboard of the film, as she did on the set of the 1961 version of *West Side Story*.

The camera pulls up and back. Dark dawn is giving way to first light, the sun breaking through a severe raking angle, revealing (. . .) rubble; block upon block, nothing but ruin and devastation, like Dresden or Hiroshima, as far as the eye can see.

Except in a lower corner of the screen, where the metal skeleton on Lincoln Center is beginning to rise.

A bell sounds somewhere on the West Side, and the final notes of "Somewhere" sound, and . . .

THE END

—from the script by Tony Kushner

ACKNOWLEDGMENTS

from author Laurent Bouzereau

This book would not have been possible without the collaboration, support, and enthusiasm of: Steven Spielberg, Kristie Macosko Krieger, and Tony Kushner.

Gustavo Dudamel, Janusz Kaminski, Michael Kahn and Sarah Broshar, Daniel Lupi, Kevin McCollum, Rita Moreno, David Newman, Justin Peck, Carla Raij, Adam Somner, Adam Stockhausen, Matt Sullivan, Paul Tazewell, Jeanine Tesori, John Williams.

Ansel Elgort, Rachel Zegler, Ariana DeBose, David Alvarez, Brian d'Arcy James, Mike Faist, Josh Andrés Rivera, Ezra Menas, and the entire cast, production team, and crew of *West Side Story*.

Unit photographer Niko Tavernese.

Nina, Jamie, and Alex Bernstein, David Saint, Stephen Sondheim, Ellen Sorrin, and Virginia Sánchez Korrol.

Master unit publicist Larry Kaplan; my documentary team, John Moers (camera), Brad Bergbom (sound).

Brittani Lindman, Clay Lerner, Emma Molz, Jack Craymer, and Jack Santell.

Christine Marx Higgins and Gina Zegler.

At Amblin Partners: Jon Anderson, Matt Andrée Wiltens, Dan Berger, Marvin Levy. And: Holly Bario, Jeb Brody, Christine Burt, Justin Falvey, Michelle Fandetti, Darryl Frank, Mark Graziano, Andrea McCall, Elizabeth Nye, Jeff Small.

Asad Ayaz, Anne Larimer Hart, Michael Mulvihill, Michael Perman, Jamie Richardson, Carol Roeder, Kathryn Ross, Michelle Sewell, Melissa Stone.

The amazing team at Abrams: Connor Leonard, Eric Klopfer, Chad W. Beckerman, Diane Shaw, and Lisa Silverman.

Mark Falkin of the Falkin Agency, Ryan McNeily at WME, Derek Kroeger.

My husband, Markus Keith; Sherri Crichton; Mark Harris, Stephanie Kluft, Ariana Topke; Kristin Stark; my parents, Daniel and Micheline Bouzereau; my sisters, Cécile and Géraldine; and longtime friend Laurent Hagége.

Editor: Connor Leonard
Designer: Chad W. Beckerman
Production Manager: Larry Pekarek
Managing Editor: Lisa Silverman
Design Manager: Diane Shaw

Library of Congress Control Number: 2020931059

ISBN: 978-1-4197-5063-2

© 2021 20th Century Studios

Printed and bound in the United States
10 9 8 7 6 5 4 3 2 1

Abrams books are available at special discounts when purchased in quantity for premiums and promotions as well as fundraising or educational use. Special editions can also be created to specification. For details, contact specialsales@abramsbooks.com or the address below. Abrams® is a registered trademark of Harry N. Abrams, Inc.

ABRAMS The Art of Books
195 Broadway, New York, NY 10007
abramsbooks.com